D1617301

the barbless HOOK

INNER SANCTUM OF ANGLING REVEALED

Dennis D. Dauble

FishHead Press, Richland, Washington

Published by:
FishHead Press
3029 Sonoran Drive
Richland, WA 99354
www.dennisdauble.com

In cooperation with:
Keokee Co. Publishing, Inc.
405 Church St
Sandpoint, ID 83864
(208) 263-3573
www.keokeebooks.com

ISBN 978-1-537187-94-5

Cover artwork by Emily Nisbet

Printed in the United State of America

"Fish worship. Is it wrong?"
Ray Troll

"The company of a madman is exhausting
even though you have somehow grown
to like him very much."
Jim Harrison

"Never go to sleep when your meat
is on the fire."
Pueblo

TABLE OF CONTENTS

Acknowledgments

LET'S START BY ADMITTING without the tolerance and understanding of family members and friends, I would have few interesting experiences from which to draw upon. I am thankful to my two older brothers who started it all by "taking me along." This act of kindness was fortunate because my dad could not read the water. But most of all, it's my late Uncle Chuck I remain grateful to for sharing his penchant to entertain with yarns about a day spent fishing.

I am indebted to my wife Nancy who carefully reviewed all 26 stories to weed out spurious content and assure proper tone where cleverness gets the best of me. Without her thoughtful insight and steadfast support throughout this project, I would not have had the freedom to operate. My sister Darcy made substantive editorial and content suggestions that improved several articles. Thank you big sister. Numerous discussions with friend and editor Georganne O'Connor helped these stories read and look like the collection I imagined it could be. Any error in grammar, judgment and fact are mine alone. The book cover and chapter art is by Emily Nisbet.

Several stories appeared in part or in slightly different form in the following publications: Yarn Gone Wild, Nights on a Boat, Odd Man Out and On Retirement in *Northwest Sportsman*; Still Smokin' and Making Fish Sausage in the *Tri-City Herald*; Closet Bait Fishermen and Swimming With Dolphins in *Washington-Oregon Game & Fish*.

"... THE WHOLE DISCOURSE IS, OR RATHER WAS,
A PICTURE OF MY OWN DISPOSITION ..."
ISAAK WALTON

PREFACE

THIS BOOK, MOSTLY ABOUT fishing for salmon and steelhead with friends, is set in my home waters: the Columbia and lower Snake rivers, inland waterways of Washington and Oregon, and streams that flow from the Blue Mountains, where I was raised. Some stories capture events that occurred over the past 10 years or so. Others are about the subconscious connection between everyday life and fishing. Some names have been changed to protect the innocent (or the guilty), particularly if character assassination might be inferred. However, in all instances (and despite careful insinuation), no malice is intended.

These stories are not about the ethereal nature of angling. Instead, they reflect drama between real people in real places and the assumptions, disagreements and feelings anglers struggle with in their quest for the biggest and most fish. Take the relationship between me and Leroy, for example. We often battle like an old married couple, but eventually make up because neither of us is willing to develop a relationship with another of equal stature. Then there's my friend Archie, and his announcement on our first fishing trip that he was a "control freak" and I should not expect to drive his boat. As a result, I don't have to concentrate on anything other than catching a fish.

At the other end of the spectrum is my soul mate Al who

turned over command of his brand-new watercraft after less than 5 minutes on the water so he could sip beer and relax. And Bob, the fourth major character in this collection is one I can always count on when I am not in the mood to be dealt a wild card.

The inner sanctum is rarely described in where-to, when-to and how-to fishing articles. It's those unstated thoughts, fears and anxieties that swirl around in your head when you fish. It's about the need to catch a fish to validate your self-worth. As a collection, the book reflects common emotions and behaviors that always have and will surface on fishing trips. You know what I mean, the conflict over things ranging from netting a fish, who controls the boat tiller and who buys the beer and donuts (or doesn't), to snubs over assumed territory, challenges involved with taking turns and the value of Smelly Jelly.

Why expose the dark side of human nature that anglers exhibit when on the water in search of the "big one?" Maybe it's because angling is easily a metaphor for life and some days on the water are often more complicated that we care to admit. No matter what your view, reflecting on behaviors can help you become a better angler, better fishing buddy and a better person. Life is too short to sulk like a sore-mouthed trout suffering from multiple hook sets. Even if the barb is removed.

Really all you can do is keep fishing.

Busted Rods and Wasted Days

THERE IS A CLASSIC Bill Dance video that shows behind-the-scenes screw-ups collected from his bass fishing shows: back-lashed reels, snakes dropping from overhanging trees, snagged lines on trolling motors and busted rods, to mention a few. A friend attached a file of this video to an e-mail message titled "Like fishing with Al and Denny"—apparently in reference to a walleye fishing trip where my fishing buddy Al broke a rod, among a few other misdeeds that included dropping a full carton of night crawlers over the side and losing two eater-sized walleye at the net.

Jigging for walleye in close proximity of friends is the type of situation that sets up for critical observation and comment. As a result, following Corey's initial e-mail was a barrage of messages about my probable role in Al's rod-breaking incident. Apparently, some so-called pals had been holding back. Archie was first to chime in, "Yup. You add those two together and rods will break."

I countered. "I find it ironic that I never break a rod in the presence of others."

Tim responded, "Ummm... The last time I fished with you up there you broke one of my spinning rods. What's that all about? Selective memory?"

Archie came back with more of the same, "He's done the same for me when we fished below McNary."

1

The more I thought about the inference behind their allegations, the more upset I got. Al broke the rod while I was at the controls of his boat. I drive Al's boat because it allows him to relax and drink Bud Light all day. In return, I get to fish where I want to. It's a win-win situation. That's how it works with fishing buddies.

My main argument was driving someone's boat does not make you responsible for them busting a rod as long as you navigate properly while they attempt to disengage their line from the bottom of the river. In my defense, I did everything a person should do. I motored slowly upstream in the general direction of Al's hang-up while he jerked like a mad man who had fished for 6 hours without receiving so much as a tick of a bite from a lethargic walleye. Sure, I felt bad that it was his brother's rod. But, those things happen. That's why experienced anglers take along a spare rod. A safe alternative would be to troll in mid-water, but good luck catching a bottom-hugging walleye.

As for Tim, I honestly had no memory of breaking his rod. We fished together maybe a handful of times. Why would I use one of his rods when I always take two or three of my own? Accordingly, I communicated such, which shut him up although it's possible that he carried on further behind my back.

Rather than do the smart thing and let it go, I continued the topic of broken rods at lunch when it was too early into the main course (a ham and double cheese sandwich) to converse about other workplace diversions, such as sex. I kept an eagle eye on Bob's body language when idle chatter drifted to how his brand new rod mysteriously broke while we fished for steelhead on the Columbia River. Bob emoted only a vacant stare when he recounted finding his new rod wedged between the starboard gunwale and my trolling motor after a short drive up the river. As I recall, one quick turn of the steering wheel had rendered it obsolete.

Again, no direct evidence of negligence on my part. Anyway, Bob is not the type of displaced Minnesotan to hold a grudge. It would be an entirely different situation if I had stepped on his favorite walleye plug.

As for Archie, I always suspected he had a bee in his bonnet after he snapped a favorite rod halfway up the butt section during a fishing trip on the Umatilla River. How could I forget the stinging remark directed to me on the drive home? "I always break a rod when I am with you."

My opinion of the incident was that jerking on 30 lb test rag line is not a good idea when you are hung up on the bottom of the river. I could have easily reminded Archie, but elected to let it go. Evidently, he was not able to reach into his heart to forgive me for something I had no part in.

Then again, Archie might have factored in another incident where I played a secondary role. On that day, an out-of-town guest snapped Archie's favorite trolling rod in half while fighting a large Chinook salmon. My contribution was netting the dropper weight instead of the salmon. Was it my fault the rod broke due to excess pressure from the tangle? Debatable. The rod was old and I was not holding it. Plus, I didn't have my best game that morning due to consuming a bowl of toxic potato soup the night before.

Or maybe it was the walleye trip downstream of McNary Dam that Archie alluded to earlier. Once again, he demonstrated the memory of an elephant, "You stepped on the tip of a rod that was laying on the floor of my boat when we fished below the freeway bridge. You postulated, after the fact, that I could have easily been the one who broke it since it was not discovered until later. However, it was on the side of the boat where you were fishing."

Archie's detailed account sparked a vague recollection of a warm summer night when we fished barefoot and shirtless until the moon came out. I caught two eater-sized walleye and he caught none. That much I remembered because I can count the number of times I have out-fished Archie on one hand. But I drew blank when it came to the busted rod.

Guilt-by-association aside, I find it disconcerting that others blame me for their misfortune. I've busted plenty of rods and never blamed anyone but myself. Like when I closed the tailgate on a rod left leaning by my truck. Or, the time I rolled up a car window with the rod tip sticking out. I've busted others doing more normal things like jerking on the bottom of a river or when hung up in a tree branch. Just last winter, I broke a rod tip while removing ice from the guides. The possibilities are unlimited.

Apparently, and unlike my fishing buddies, I was raised to not cry over spilled milk. I have learned that a quality rod can be sent back to manufacturers with a pitiful note and replaced for a nominal fee. Or the intact piece saved with other miscellaneous rod parts for recycling. Consider my growing stack behind the hot water heater. As a recent example of resourcefulness, I spliced a loose tip from an old trolling rod onto a sturgeon rod that had previously succumbed to a soft spot in graphite composition. The makeshift rod isn't pretty but it picks up aggressive bites. And just last week, I married up a nice IM-6 rod. The green butt section clashes with its mocha brown mate, but the rod casts like brand new.

There is little else to add to this complicated topic. Rods will break and fishermen will blame others if there is the slightest glimmer of complicity. I can only hope my fishing buddies will learn to forgive and forget before I run the table with the whole sniveling bunch.

ODD MAN OUT

ᑋ

BEING ODD MAN OUT is deeply ingrained in my persona due to being the third manchild in a family of five children. Such lack of offspring symmetry led to complication at discount motels during my formative years. With my parents having one bed, my sisters the other and my older brothers sharing the fold-down couch, I was left to spend a restless night on the floor. I never complained because it was a better arrangement than overnight stays with friends who slept three to a bed like hillbillies.

The process for parceling out fried chicken at the dinner table created another challenge for a large odd-numbered family. It's well known that every major edible part of a chicken comes in pairs. I bring this fact up, because it was the one time that I came out ahead. Again, distribution hierarchy of resources prevailed with mom and dad getting breast meat, my brothers the thighs, and my sisters the drumsticks. Default, not design, left me with two wings, the best part of any barnyard bird.

But I digress. This story is about being odd man out to save money if willing to sleep on a kitchen floor, wake up to a snoring duet or share elevation with a dog scratching fleas. It's about having a sore neck because of a shortage of pillows. It's about taking the last (cold) shower. All are common occurrences on fishing trips when an extra person is brought in to share a room.

The most recent incident took place during a spring fishing trip for pre-spawning walleye. Our off-season room with two doubles at the Sky Deck Motel in Electric City, Washington was a bargain at $65 per night. The shared cost dropped even more when my buddy Al asked to squeeze in his younger brother Andy. Reflecting on childhood experience, I figured to sleep on the floor. However, since they wanted to fish out of my boat things worked in my favor. I got first choice of beds. Andy got the air mattress and the floor.

An early check-in assured a strategic placement of my bed sans a view of the vanity and mirror. I had previously been burned in such a manner while salmon fishing in Alaska. Imagine starting off a day with a "Full-Monty" view of a motel-mate's backside. (Hint: It had something to do with sleeping in a rollaway cot wedged up next to the vanity sink.) First guy up has bathroom privileges, sure, but wearing skivvies while brushing one's teeth is only polite. How did I get in this predicament? Because I was willing to be the odd man in order to save money! In "hindsight," I'd gladly have paid twice what I saved to purge the image of those pasty wrinkled butt cheeks from my head.

Back to the walleye trip. Things were calm around the motel the first night. We walked up the hill to the bar for an evening of burgers and shuffleboard. There were no fistfights, alcohol consumption was minimal and we left early to be on the water by sunup. Nobody snored and nobody passed gas, although Al woke us up at 3 a.m. yelling obscenities in his sleep.

Atmosphere around the motel was markedly different the second night when a group of boisterous trout anglers showed up. They bragged about the number of triploids they caught and we responded with lies about 10 pound walleye. Satisfactory primal greetings exchanged we merrily washed down grilled sausage, smoked fish and elk jerky with cheap beer and blended whiskey. It was well after midnight before we staggered back to our room. No alarm was set. A breakfast menu was not discussed. Walleye could wait.

Apparently the party was not over for all. I had barely fallen asleep when a drunken man running around our room awakened me. The first sign of something out of the ordinary was cold wind blowing through a wide-open front door. The second was a naked form illuminated by the glare of the front porch light. Before I could yell a warning, the intruder jumped on Al and Andy's bed (It was originally Al's bed, but seems that Andy crawled in, hillbilly style, because his air mattress deflated). Our latest roommate rolled around on top of the bed covers, cackling loudly over their combined and fervent protests. Meanwhile, I pulled a bed sheet over my head for protection from the unseemly visual assault. The bare-ass bandit eventually ran out the door, but only after planting a sloppy kiss on Al's forehead and proclaiming, "I love you, man."

As I recall, this remarkable incident was the only time—other than eating fried chicken—that an odd man arrangement worked to my advantage.

On Trespassing, Poaching and Other Nefarious Acts

$\textbf{\biggl\downharpoonleft}$

WHETHER IT'S EXCEEDING the speed limit, listing extra charitable contributions at tax time, rounding down a pound of nails at the hardware store or bagging an extra donut from the self-serve bakery, some people think they can beat the system. These behaviors describe my big brother, who along with many others, can't seem to stay on the straight and narrow. And as you might expect, these behaviors can extend to the trout stream.

Dusty's list of excuses for keeping a decent-sized trout hooked in any body part besides the mouth is longer than the wild hair on my right eyebrow. Other slight-of-hand maneuvers have included slipping extra fish into the side pocket of his vest and stretching the backbone of undersized specimens. Given proclivity to bend rules and regulations, it's not surprising that he occasionally harvests from a catch-and-release area. And while he hasn't figured out how to beat the adipose-clip challenge, the topic of Super Glue as a wound sealer has come up.

I try not to hold these infractions against him. They're too minor to merit being sent to the Big House. Plus, he is my brother and forgiveness is divine. He who is without sin shall cast the first worm into "Fly-Fishing Only" water and all that. However, a few of the more civilly disobedient incidents have stuck in my craw. A classic case followed a day of salmon fishing on the Alsea

River in western Oregon. While scrambling up the bank, I heard a vehicle drive by and stop on the county road that paralleled the river. Dusty sent me ahead because he didn't have a catch card. It turned out to be a smart move because the driver was a game cop. I played it cool by pulling out my fishing license and talking loud. Meanwhile, Dusty stayed safely hidden in the deep brush. If you think lying to your mother is tough, try lying to a uniformed man wearing 17-inch-high black boots and packing a pistol.

Then there was the time we fished for steelhead on the Walla Walla River near the Whitman Mission. It was another in a long series of trips where my brother showed up "a little light" on gear. To translate, this phrase means he lacks essentials such as split shot, hooks and corkies. Oh yes, I also supplied the bait. Knowing that we were well outside his home state, I asked if he had purchased a non-resident fishing license. Given other shortcomings, it was no surprise when he replied, "Didn't have time to get one."

I knew my big brother was cheap, but figured the real reason for him not procuring a license was he figured the odds of getting caught were low. The trick was on him, however, when we returned to find a deputy sheriff standing by my truck. Turns out an irate farmer didn't like where we had parked and had called in a complaint. The deputy, sufficiently frustrated after driving back-and-forth looking for us for over an hour, was poised to write a ticket.

Luckily I produced a "Feel-free-to-fish" slip signed by an adjacent landowner. This piece of information calmed the deputy down, but he still insisted on doing paperwork so I provided my fishing license. He scrawled the facts in a little green note pad before turning to my brother. There was no doubt in my mind that my sibling would finally be paying the piper. But to my amazement, when the sheriff asked for a fishing license, Dusty mumbled, "I was just along."

Just along? I was stunned. Dusty had river water dripping off his hip boots. His fishing vest was stained with old roe and he held a fully rigged spinning rod in his right hand. The bright red corkie I had so generously loaned him swung hypnotically on slack line below his rod tip.

More amazing was this bogus answer was good enough for a back-up law enforcement official stuck working a holiday weekend. In fact, the county's finest didn't bother looking up to challenge or acknowledge the nefarious statement. As far as the law was concerned, it was case closed. Slipping the little green note pad back into his shirt pocket, the deputy drove off in search of a jelly donut.

I've got more big brother stories. Recently, Dusty drove 100 miles to the Deschutes River only to find his favorite fly-fishing stretch posted up like a fortress. Knowing there would be no dinner unless he bagged a fat trout, he snuck through a locked gate and commenced to cast big MF hairy-winged stoneflies at rising redside rainbows. Unfortunately, a security guard paid by a bunch of rich guys to patrol for anglers unable to afford four-figure annual dues detected his presence.

Dusty recounted the adventure pragmatically. "It was the gatekeeper (that caught me). He kept driving back and forth up on the road so I laid down in the weeds to hide. It was a half hour before I could sneak out to the main road and get away."

Am I missing something? Was I the only member of the family who paid attention to stories about baby Jesus? It would seem so, except that my brother is not alone in what constitutes trespassing. A primary criterion of most anglers (consistent with other violations of the law) seems to be the likelihood of being caught. That's why certain factors, such as proximity to dwellings and sign of human activity come into play when one decides to venture on the backside of a "No Trespassing" sign.

There are obvious deterrents to casual exploring on private property, for example, 8-foot-high electric fences or concertina wire strung up like bubble lights at a Christmas pageant. Another clue the welcome wagon is not around is a regular spaced line-up of brand-new "No Trespassing" signs tacked to fence posts. There should be no argument in these situations. Someone does not want you to fish on their property!

All that aside, lurking somewhere below the most blatant transgressions are various categories of denial. These are gray areas where conduct is subject to interpretation. My two favorite points of view involving private access are "This sign ain't meant for me" and "Access is for the beholder." Such interpretation is typically applied to locations you have fished before. It has to do with entitlement. My brother is not alone in this behavior. Much like migrating salmon, every red-blooded American returns to home ground. One difference is that for humans, familiarity can breed defilement. Or something like that.

Rules of engagement are not so obvious when you encounter a streamside sign blocking access to your favorite fishing hole. If the sign is placed perpendicular to the shoreline, do you go back? Or is it legal to go around the sign if you stay below the high water mark? Consider the navigable stream rule. Rumor is, for any stream large enough to float a boat, the river bottom is open to the general public. In other words, you ain't trespassing if you keep your boots in the water. These options go through your mind.

Once as a test, I asked my friend Archie what he would do

when faced with this situation. His answer was classic avoidance. "I usually wade to the other side of the river and keep fishing."

Bingo! The truth is that there are more variations in how anglers respond to rules and regulations than there are beer bellies in an Irish pub. As for my big brother, there might be hope. Just the other day he asked if he should crimp down the barb on the fly I recently lent him. My heart swelled with pride although I did not recollect him pulling out needle nose pliers to comply with the barbless hook regulation. Regardless, it's the thought that counts. Everyone has to start someplace.

Managing Expectation

$\cup$

GIVEN CHOICE OF ANY angling venue, I would rather wade streams in pursuit of steelhead than anything else in the world. This affliction has as much to do with the nature of the setting as the fighting qualities of the species. The rub, or should I say the itch that needs scratching, is when a prideful need to validate the experience leads to lowering of standards. An effective rationalization being that this fly fisher has to occasionally slum to know the difference.

On one such slumming occasion, I pulled into the fish hatchery complex at Lyons Ferry to meet up with my fishing buddy Leroy who had been there since before first light. The scene was desolate. Low fog hung over frozen ground puddled from an early morning drizzle. A steady southwest wind pushed whitecaps against the basalt riprap shoreline. The only thing setting the surface of the lower Snake River apart from a dull winter landscape was the motion of water.

Navigating a series of speed bumps, I threaded past narrow concrete raceways covered with black mesh netting, one-story corrugated metal buildings, the hatchery manager's house and a sagging double-wide trailer. Two vehicles were in the angler's parking lot located at the west end of it all. One was an aged Ford Courier. Peering expectantly out the driver's side window was a small monkey-faced dog. The other vehicle was Leroy's familiar blue-and-white long bed Ford F-250. I collected my fishing gear and walked over to check out the river.

When I looked down the steep dirt bank to where Leroy stood clad in full rain gear, he turned and shook his head slowly from side-to-side. "Looks like a big goose egg."

I replied, "Don't bring me down. I just got here."

That's one problem with pessimists. They often dwell on worst case hoping to be better prepared when a bad thing happens. When I reminded Leroy of this detail, he smiled and said, "Got to manage your expectation."

Our fishing relationship could be loosely characterized as a pair of old men too self-centered to fish with others except on special occasion. We are default fishing partners thrown together because our children have grown up and we imagine that it would be informative or social to fish with another person on occasion. What Leroy and I have in common is a passion for fishing. Most any kind of fishing. What we don't have in common is similar sleeping habits.

Accordingly, the arrangement settled on over a lengthy phone call the evening before was to meet at the hatchery. That I don't stir until well after the rooster crows can push the start of a winter fishing day to mid-morning. In contrast, Leroy wakes up before dawn, rain or shine, work or play, spring or fall. More important, he chomps at the bit if he has to wait for me. Driving separate vehicles to a shared fishing destination—even when it means a lonely commute—is standard default when proposed starting times conflict. Sometimes dealing with differences is easier than forcing compromise.

The occasion called for dangling dyed bait shrimp below a slip bobber. Shrimp and bobber fishing is a widely practiced sport by steelhead anglers who don't have a boat, lack the leg strength to wade streams or don't know the difference. My fly fisher pals consider the approach one of the more demeaning forms of fishing, but the freezer was empty and my two favorite tributary streams were running high and muddy from snow melt. While I was concerned certain purist-minded individuals might find out about this bait-fishing trip, the odds were slim. And if they did, I would be forced to remind them of such things as strike indicators, plastic beads, Flesh Flies and Glo-Bugs.

All excuses aside, premeditation was involved. I brought along a brand-new wooden casting bobber purchased specifically for the occasion. It was a thing of beauty: just under 8 inches long and painted in consecutive black, white, yellow and neon orange stripes. I planned to mooch the rest of the gear off Leroy.

Leroy's early arrival had secured the uppermost casting station near the hatchery, a premier location closest to a "No Fishing" zone established downstream of an outfall pipe. The idea is juvenile steelhead released from the Lyons Ferry hatchery will loiter near this natal water source when they return as adults. There were several other openings where bank side willow had been removed to allow two people to stand shoulder-to-shoulder. The river bottom dropped off gradually from the rip rap shoreline to about 15-feet depth. Current was gentle, backed up from Lower Monumental Dam.

When Leroy sensed hesitation in my approach to rig the slip bobber, he barked directions like a drill sergeant. "Tie on the bobber stop first, then add a plastic bead, corkie, bobber, another plastic bead, then a swivel. Finally, tie your hook and leader to the swivel."

Desperately trying to commit the sequence to memory, I rustled through his rusty tackle box for parts. When I messed up by sliding on a second bead after the barrel swivel, Leroy admonished, "It won't work that way. Even a 6-year old knows how to string up a slip bobber," giving a knowing nod to a young lady who only recently had arrived with her father to fish near us.

I owned up to using the technique too infrequently to get the hang of it, but Leroy ignored me while keeping an eye on his bobber, until I messed up again. "How many times do I have to tell you that the bobber comes after the second bead!" he said.

Absorbing the blow like a well-trained sparring partner, I finally constructed my rig. Without waiting for approval, I pilfered a fat purple-dyed shrimp from Leroy's plastic bait container, cinched it onto the shaft of my #2 barbless hook and winged a long cast into a slight breeze. "Jesus. That bobber hit like a bomb. You're scaring the fish away!" Leroy yelled.

During empty moments between a long series of unrewarded casts Leroy expounded on the many nuances of bobber fishing for steelhead. He reminded his synthetic line floated while my monofilament sunk. Sinking led to slack line, a feature that compromised one's ability to set the hook on a hungry steelhead. Another pearl of wisdom bestowed was that un-weighted bobbers (such as his) lay flat when not fishing properly. In contrast, my big-butted casting bobber provided no such hint that anything was wrong below the surface. Leroy also informed me that pinching large split shot directly above the hook rather than at the swivel imparted more attractive motion to shrimp. I soaked these facts up like a sponge and tried to remain alert to all possible changes in behavior of my indifferent bobber.

Leroy eventually got bored with bobber-fishing and began to chuck a #4 rainbow-colored Vibrax along the shoreline. I couldn't help but notice it was one of fifteen identical spinners in his tackle box, lending support to a standard operating philosophy for many anglers: you can never have too much of a good thing. Meanwhile, I adjusted my bobber to put my shrimp at 6 feet below the surface and was rewarded with a quick takedown that I missed. "You sure are lucky when you bobber fish," Leroy said. "Next time, you might consider hooking a fish."

Hoping to have the option of bumming shrimp for the rest of my bobber-fishing life, I replied, "My success has to do with your excellent bait."

What followed next was almost bizarre. My bobber began to move slowly yet surely upstream, plowing through the water like it was balanced on a muskrat's nose. "Set the hook you idiot!" Leroy yelled.

Although the scene was hypnotic, I managed to snap out of the trance to jerk my rod. Unfortunately, I set the hook just as my line crossed Leroy's. Given such tight quarters, our rods clashed like we were fencing. To make matters worse, Leroy tangled me up with his spinner when he reeled in. It was no surprise that the fish got off while we struggled to undo the mess. "What was that all about?" I mumbled, hoping to dissolve the ridiculousness of the event.

"All I know is that twice you've had take-downs and missed and now you had a fish suck your bait down and swim halfway to the hatchery and you didn't hook it either," Leroy said.

We spent the next 2 hours watching our bobbers drift slowly downstream and replacing shrimp that got their heads torn off by peamouth chub that lived year-round near the hatchery. My fingers smelled like week-old ceviche and my right shirtsleeve was bright red from handling dyed shrimp.

At mid-morning, a freight train pulling a long procession of cars scraped and whined its way over the quarter-mile-long steel-girder bridge that spanned the Snake River near the confluence of the Palouse River. The conductor blew his whistle sharply three times before the train turned downstream along the opposite shore. A black plume of diesel smoke trailed over freight cars loaded with lumber and wheat for overseas markets. Imagining the vibration of those big steel wheels might stimulate a bite from a nervous steelhead, I stole one of Leroy's best shrimp while he was train watching and cast out as far as I could. "Time for a lo-co-mo-tive bite!" I yelled.

Wouldn't you know but my fancy wooden bobber went under before it drifted 10 feet. I frantically reeled in a long bow of slack line before attempting to set the hook. Unfortunately, the bobber re-surfaced without a steelhead attached. I was now 0 for 3 with takedowns, and it felt like the whole world was counting.

You've certainly had your chances, but, I don't feel sorry for you." Leroy said.

"I wouldn't expect much sympathy since you haven't had even so much as a nibble yet. Tell the truth, have you ever felt sorry for me?"

Leroy didn't waste a breath. "I can remember feeling that way once."

"When was that?" I said. "I would like a point of reference."

"Well, if you must know, it was off the Okanogan River when you lost your downrigger off the side of the boat and then lost the salmon."

"I almost had forgotten the part about losing the salmon," I said. "I do remember that you weren't much help and that I had to fight the fish with one hand while reeling up the downrigger with the other. I wasn't happy when the downrigger ended up in the bottom of the river. But, losing the salmon put the frosting on the cake."

"You sat on the back of the boat with your head down after the salmon got off. I did feel a little sorry for you, although you handled it well."

"What I remembered about that particular fiasco was that I caught more salmon trolling with an old-style banana sinker than you did using the spare downrigger. Funny, I don't remember feeling sorry for you when you netted my salmon," I added, to ensure we didn't get too carried away with sensibility.

Time passed. More time passed. No action anywhere and we were both getting bored. It's not good to be bored while steelhead fishing. After holding on to his rod for nearly 5 hours straight Leroy announced, "I'm taking a break."

He made a long cast and propped his rod on a log. But before he could count to 10, his bobber disappeared, surfaced and went down again. "Got it," Leroy boasted, standing up to set the hook. "That's how you catch them."

I reeled in, feeling more than a little remorse at this cruel twist of fate. After a brief tussle, Leroy horsed a small, dark hatchery steelhead to shore. "Get the net," he commanded, invocating the tone of a storm trooper.

I complied, but only after loitering long enough to let him know who was in charge. "That was a pathetic fight plus the fish ain't that good-looking," I said, as he led the compliant steelhead into the open net.

"It's better than getting skunked. Want it? My freezer is full."

"Why not?" I replied, anticipating ample time to rationalize the deprecating affair on the long drive home. Plus, the steelhead would smoke up fine, regardless of who caught it or the method of enticement. After all, one has to manage expectation.

Taking Turns

THERE WAS A TIME I wouldn't order fish when dining out. I didn't care if it was a four-star restaurant. If I didn't catch it, I wouldn't eat it. Paying a guide to show me how to catch a fish was even farther out of the question. Until recently, I also shunned charter boats as a fishing experience you could take little credit for.

But now, I'm able to rationalize the value of paying for a spot on a boat. There's an unanticipated break in a business trip when opportunity presents itself. Or on family vacation when my boat's home, but I need one to get to where fish are biting. I've found these impromptu trips can range from interesting to disastrous depending on clientele and crew.

Sometimes, charter trips are managed well, but often they are not. Some captains, it seems, prefer a "hands off" approach, while others could be writing up procedural manuals for a major corporation. My worst charter experience was a $500 trip trolling for marlin off the west coast of Maui. We weren't 15 minutes out of the harbor before the hung-over captain retreated to a sleeping berth never to emerge until we approached the dock 6 hours later. The bait boy did his best to get us a fish but the trip was nothing more than a cruise in the deep blue sea.

One trip for halibut out of Westport, Washington, demonstrated the value of knowing specified rules of engagement.

Eighteen of us rubes boarded the 51-foot "Maria." The high number of anglers led to a need to prevent lines from entangling, so only nine were allowed to fish at one time. The way it worked was the first nine guys to write their names on a signup sheet in the main cabin were in the first group to drop bait. Experienced charter boat fishermen arrive early and look for such a signup sheet. This charter novice figured out the process in time to write my name on line #18. Consequently, I had to wait with hands in my pockets until nine halibut were landed before I was allowed to touch a rod.

That's one version of waiting for your turn. I managed my big boy feelings because complaining would have only made me look dumber than I felt for not knowing about the signup sheet. It also helped that I landed a halibut before three guys who signed up before me.

There's more on the chicken soup topic of taking turns, with the common denominator being trolling. Not trolling with a rod in your hand, but hands-off trolling that involves watching and waiting for a strike from a rod glued to a rod-holder. Two recent guided trips provided an entirely different, and much more sophisticated approach, to taking turns, both proving it's hard to manage your feelings (and play nice) when getting the short end of the deal.

Trip number one involved fishing for albacore off the Oregon Coast. Six good friends booked a charter boat out of Depoe Bay. The agreed-upon plan was first-time anglers would have first shot at a tuna. After everyone put a tuna in the box, we would rotate through the group until we had two apiece. It was then on to fish number three and beyond until there was a giant pile of bloody tuna on the deck. That was the idea anyway. Everyone would have fair opportunity to land an equal number of fish regardless of their angling ability or position at the rail.

My friend Bob and I had come home from Westport the year before with 50 pounds of tuna loins. As a result, we opted out of the action until the first four fish were brought to the boat. Neither of us had a problem with the arrangement mainly because we anticipated little standby time. But, as the day unfolded, things were not as straightforward as imagined.

The taking turns plan was fairly congenial through round one. If two pair of hands met around a rod butt, there was no violent exchange of "Screw you!" One person retreated politely for a try at the next fish. Still, an undercurrent of discontent began to surface, providing an edge to the conversation after the first hour or so. Those waiting for a turn began to critique the skills of those fighting a fish, which led to verbal sparring whether hooking and losing a fish should count as a turn. In the end, the tuna rookies were allowed a second and third chance to catch a fish if they messed up a hook-set or if they lost a fish at the rail. After all, we had several hours of fishing and a boatload of tuna in front of us.

Action was sufficiently slow that keeping track of the number of tuna was not a challenge. Bob and I soon realized that speed trolling around the perimeter of a school of feeding tuna with multi-colored skirted jigs was nowhere as effective as fishing with live bait—our previous tuna experience. And, as with any guided trip having a low catch rate, we couldn't help but be concerned that the cost per pound of fresh albacore filets was not decreasing fast enough to compensate for time and money spent.

Unfortunately, it was noon before we figured out the skipper was a better boat driver than a guide. The first hint was his 120-gallon capacity cooler—small by charter boat standards—with four bags of grocery story ice. The second hint was when I overheard him asking Corey's opinion on what could be done to get more hook-ups.

Despite these shortcomings, we remained vigilant, constantly searching the sea surface for signs of feeding tuna and sea birds. Once a school of albacore was located, the boat captain trolled through the heart of it, but we seldom hooked more than one fish per pass. By mid-afternoon we'd managed to work 30 miles offshore and boat a grand total of 15 tuna. I was anxious for more action and I was not alone.

Because of the taking turns arrangement, three of us were stuck on two tuna apiece. It didn't matter that we six friends enjoyed each other's company and would split the loins equally at the end of the day. I had been willing to let bygones be bygones, but with less than an hour of fishing time left, there would be no more Mister Nice Guy. I was going to the mat for the next takedown. I would not be deprived of tuna number three. And I couldn't help but reflect I wouldn't be in such a precarious position if we had made a rule to move everyone who hooked and lost a fish to the back of the line. They would have been benched for poor performance in any other team sport.

Bob, Kyle and I stood shoulder-to-shoulder across the aft of the boat positioning ourselves to grab the next rod that went off. The rest of the group relaxed in the main cabin. Finally, the back port rod, a reliable one most of the day, went off with a hard strike followed by tight line and a screeching reel. What followed was a violent rendition of musical chairs. The three of us crashed together in our haste to pull the bent rod out of its holder. Luckily, I had the inside position and managed to wrestle the rod away. "Sorry," I said, but I didn't mean it.

I wasted little time bringing my third and last tuna of the day to the boat to be gaffed. It was now down to two desperate anglers, Bob and Kyle, who roamed the deck like basketball players positioning for the tip, eyes darting left then right, watching for a rod to go off. Finally, a tuna struck. Bob, the wily veteran, out-dueled a frantic Kyle, who took a face-plant into the rail while giving it his all. Bob then milked the fight like it was his last fish of the day, which it was. Mercifully, the captain allocated extra trolling time for Kyle to get his third tuna.

Fishing shouldn't have to be that complicated. But it is. Take a competitive situation like group fishing and add the twist of taking turns and there will be conflict. Mix in the fact that guided trips ain't cheap and everyone wants their money's worth. Not to mention that bragging about the biggest and the most fish happens and no one wants to be left out of that conversation. Hardly the setting for a definitive path to fair play let alone its implementation. As I think about it, even in simpler situations things don't always turn out fair. There's always the teacher's pet and just plain luck that will reward the undeserving too.

Given the Depoe Bay tuna-fishing experience, I should have known better than to sign up for another guided trip. But I didn't. I joined two friends to fish for spring Chinook salmon with a guide who would show us where to fish after which we would fish out of Leroy's boat using our own gear. But plans changed when the guide offered up a half-price afternoon trip prior to our all-day trip. Why haul a boat 500 miles for a day on the water when we could book a guide for little more than the price of a tank of gasoline? Once again, rugged individualism was set aside.

The decision looked brilliant when we arrived to find boat trailers triple-parked in every available spot along the 5-acre parking lot leading from the main highway to the launch. It was urban fishing of the likes we had never seen. We found a parking spot for Leroy's truck, watched clouds sail by and admired the steady number of salmon brought in to the launch. Let somebody else drive the boat.

Our guide returned to the launch at noon with limits for his four clients. By all appearances, it looked to be a good day. He fired up his 150 horse-power Mercury jet pump and we blasted down river to the freeway bridge that connected downtown Portland to Vancouver. Milling around like a flock of coots on a farm pond were 40 or 50 other boats. The guide cut the motor to idle before explaining how we would troll cut plug herrings behind a flasher using a 10-oz dropper weight. "The guy in the back lets out 75 feet of line and the guy in the front 65 feet," he said, pointing to the line counter on our level-wind Shimano reels. "This keeps lines from getting tangled."

I favored the back of the boat so went there to start. I dutifully checked my herring to make sure it had a tight spin, let line out until the banana weight hit bottom and put my chosen rod in its holder. Other than occasionally tangling my gear with Leroy's by free-spooling line out too fast, things went well. Trolling was relatively easy due to a smooth sand bottom. There was not much to do but watch our rod tips while the guide maintained a slow weave through the loose collection of boats. The scene was not tranquil, however. Some boats motored across our path. Others flat-lined over our heads or blocked drifts by anchoring in the channel.

On the second long drift downstream of the bridge, Leroy yelled I had a bite. (He's always been better at watching my rod than I.) I jumped up from my swivel chair to grab the rod. "Not yet," our guide directed. "Let him chomp on it for 5 seconds, then reel up tight, but don't jerk to set the hook."

When the guide nodded his head, I grabbed the pulsating

rod and cranked on the reel. "It's off," he said, when my rod tip straightened.

I ignored and kept reeling until I felt the pressure of a strong fish. "It was swimming toward me!" I yelled.

The guide took his hand off the tiller and went for the net as my chrome-bright salmon danced on top of the water surface. Several long runs later, it came to the boat. The springer was slab-sided and so fresh that sea lice clung to its vent. I took a deep breath and collapsed on the bottom of the boat to fill out my punch card.

Leroy and Dan chorused, "Our turn now."

They were thrilled to have me out of the equation for the afternoon. That's the bad part of a one-fish limit. Catch a fish and you are done fishing for the day. Still basking in the glow of my first springer of the season, I anticipated how good a beer would taste when my fishing partners tagged out.

However, it wasn't to be. Although Leroy and Dan both experienced solid takedowns during the next two hours of trolling, their fish got off after short runs. Then before we knew it, it was 6 p.m. and the guide announced, "Time to reel in."

Thus, day one went into the books with only one salmon in the boat. Little did I suspect my good luck would backfire and lead to more drama the next day.

As Leroy explained later that evening when we got ready for bed, "Dan and I get first shot at a salmon tomorrow. You have to wait until we both catch one before you get to fish. It's only fair. After all, you already have one to take home."

I was speechless. But before I could protest, he continued, "This trip is not like when you and I are fishing together and we get to keep what we catch ourselves. We're all in this together. There is no real skill involved since all we do is let our line out to whatever depth the guide tells us, put our rods in a holder and wait for a take down."

"Agreed with the skill in hooking part," I replied, "but what if you guys keep losing fish like you did this afternoon? Does that mean I have to stand around all day without a chance at another fish? Why am I penalized for catching the only salmon?"

After all, I paid for a full day's fishing, the same as them. I should have been allowed to fish until I tagged out, not sit on my butt doing nothing.

"That's the way the chips fall," Leroy said. "You might concentrate on us getting a fish. Then, you'll get your chance."

I bit my lip but couldn't help reflect that his plan sucked. It's not like I would have kept all the fish for myself even if I were the only one lucky enough to punch my card twice. I suspected it was Leroy's idea. Dan was too nice a guy to gang up on someone he fished with for the first time. It's one thing if I had offered up the plan. It's a different situation when Leroy imposed it on me with no prior discussion.

I lay on my back staring at the ceiling wondering when my buddies decided to bench me. After all, we had been together most of the night. Maybe it was in the bar when a middle-aged businesswoman having a three-martini lisp and wearing a low-cut sweater engaged us in conversation? There was no stopping her once she found out we had been out fishing. Leaning into me with alcohol-laced breath, she described a recent float tube experience that I still have difficulty reconstructing. "I hooked something on my back cast, felt tension on the retrieve forward and slung it back over my head. It was a 2- to 3-foot long sturgeon so I kept it and ate it."

Or maybe their clandestine conversation took place after the bleary-eyed blonde asked Leroy if he was Norwegian? Not to be deterred when he replied "German," she looked at him with as much intensity as her alcohol-induced stupor allowed and re-marked, "You would look good in lederhosen."

I knew things were getting out of hand when she squinted at Dan to proclaim that he would look good in a kilt. Needless to say, I exited for the restroom before further ethnic wardrobe makeovers were directed at me.

Several friends were surprised when I shared the conversa-tion about Leroy's taking turns protocol. My logical comeback about sharing the catch and continuing to take turns on day two seemed reasonable to them. I didn't have a good answer why I agreed other than to keep the peace. Dwelling on my options did not lead to a good nights sleep. That and the fact hotel guests roamed the hallways until 2 a.m. while Leroy babbled nonsense in his sleep. It didn't help my mood that Leroy groaned loudly well before the alarm was to go off. I've shared enough rooms with him to know that groaning is his way of announcing readi-ness to get up and turn the room lights on.

The dawn sky was ominous with dark storm clouds over whitecaps when we arrived at the launch. Rain gear and snacks were dutifully loaded in the boat prior to the half-mile, kidney-jarring run to the I-5 Bridge. I perched on the bow seat, resigned to my fate, trying to project enthusiasm for the proceedings.

Leroy had the first takedown from one of his two assigned rods, but the fish was off before he could pick up to reel. Not long after, Dan also had a shot at a fish that he lost. I kept my hands in my pockets, back hunkered to the wind, watching and waiting for a turn. No matter how hard I tried, I could not conjure up good thoughts. Their failure was "just deserved" in my opinion.

An hour passed before Leroy experienced a successful hook-set. Unfortunately (or fortunately depending on your perspective), the fish came to the boat with not much of a fight. "They sometimes lose track of where they are first thing in the morning," the guide said.

Still, landing the salmon led to jubilation all around. Leroy was happy to rid himself of a skunk. I was happy that Leroy had nothing to grouse about. And Dan was happy for his future chances. "My turn next!" he crowed.

"Your odds are certainly good with four rods out," Leroy replied, reinforcing the code of all for one.

But Dan's ill-fated luck continued when he hooked and lost another salmon. Little wonder he was feeling snake-bit after losing three straight. Meanwhile, I was getting more impatient by the minute. It's easy to be critical of others when you have a fish in the box and they don't.

Finally, Dan hooked a salmon that stayed on. Other than snapping his 10-foot, heavy-action G Loomis in half at the midpoint of the battle, things worked out fine, at least on a pass-fail basis. "You high-sticked it," our guide said to a chagrined Dan. "Next time, try not to lift the rod so high when the fish is in close. Don't worry, the blank probably had a weak spot."

Dan cheered up after I confided the rod came with a lifetime replacement warrantee. "Pay that much and they send you a new one no matter how many times you break it."

I felt better that both Leroy and Dan had finally caught a salmon, but the best part was in knowing they were done fishing for the day. It was time for them to see how it felt to sit and do nothing while somebody else fished. As for me, there would be no more watching while detached from the action like some toga-clad eunuch in a Roman bathhouse. I joked about catching a wild salmon so that I could keep fishing for a keeper, but the humor was lost on my fishing mates.

The same lucky rod went down soon after we returned to the north shore drift. Once again, I followed the 5-second rule, waiting for the salmon to choke down the herring while everyone shouted instruction like I was developmentally challenged. Before I cranked the reel handle five times, the guide said, "It's off."

"You said that last time," I replied, reeling like crazy to catch up with a fast-moving fish. "I hate to tell you but it's still on and it's already at the boat."

Leroy and Dan shouted with glee as my salmon was quickly netted and bonked to submission. I basked in the glow of success, imagining they were happy for me. However, they offered no congratulation on a job well done, no back slap or high five. I might as well have been invisible when they moved with focused precision to the back swivel seats and began to let out line. "I thought we were done for the day," I said. "Let's head out and drink some beer."

"Sorry, our guide said we could catch his fish," Leroy replied.

"Oh, I see how it works now. Do I get a piece?"

"No. Dan and I are going to split it. You already have two fish."

Seems they had concocted up this deal while I concentrated on other matters. As explained to me while we made a run upriver, whoever got the guide's salmon would share it with the other. The fact I got my second fish allowed them to implement the plan. I couldn't help be reminded of the time my late Aunt Margaret snuck dried dates into my breakfast oatmeal and made me eat the entire bowl like there was nothing wrong. The point being it doesn't take much to transform a normal experience to something that leaves a bad taste in your mouth.

Best friends or not, individual pride was on the line for this last salmon. No matter that little skill was involved when trolling hands off with rods in a holder. No matter that all four rigs were set to a depth dictated by the guide's tried-and-true formula for catching springers. No matter the guide baited their hooks and drove the boat at exactly 2.1 mph downstream along a set GPS track. No matter all they had to do was sit until a fish struck after which they would wait for the guide to signal when to pick up the rod. What mattered now was whoever got the last fish would be fully redeemed for getting skunked on day one. The flip side was the other would have to live with catching the fewest number of fish. Not that the other two of us would ever bring it up on the long drive home.

"You take those two rods and I'll take these two," Leroy said to Dan, pointing to the port and starboard sides of the boat, respectively.

Dan nodded to the affirmative, picking the first seat next to where the guide stood at the tiller. That's when things got serious. There was no teamwork, no jive talk, no eye contact between what were now fierce competitors. Leroy and Dan appeared frozen on point, eyes only for their assigned rods. The battle was on. It was sudden death or sudden victory.

You could have cut the tension with a dull Buck knife, however the guide took little notice of the drama unfolding before him. He stood calmly at the tiller, as he had done all morning, sunglasses smattered by drops of rain and baseball hat pulled down tight.

Dan experienced a strike in the next troll sequence, but once again he failed to get a good hook set. Leroy offered no condolences. He took a deep breath to calm and repositioned like an Olympic sprinter after a false start: both hands resting lightly on his knees, feet parallel to the gunwales, eyes to the back of the boat.

Sensing a pod of springers in the vicinity, our guide motored back to the shadow of the bridge. Dan had no sooner placed his second rod in the holder when the tip went down violently. This fish was well-hooked. Fighting the salmon like he was afraid to break the rod led to a lengthy and exciting battle for Dan that was not pretty to watch. Given a free rein, the largest salmon of the trip ran circles around and under the boat until it was finally netted.

I should have felt glad for a great day, but I didn't. Instead, I was relieved the trip was over. Although things did not turn out exactly even-steven for the play, the catch was as equitable as possible under the circumstances. But best of all, there would be no more secret deals and no more taking turns.

If there is one thing to be learned from these types of trips it's that angler behavior is far too complicated to be regulated by playground rules. There is no sure way to eliminate the angst involved with a bad day of fishing, particularly when one shells out large wads of cash. As far as easing the situation by taking turns, it's far easier said than done. Even among the best of friends.

Peanut Machines

ᘰ

CALL ME SNOOPY or call me observant, but idle time spent in the lobby of a neighborhood automotive repair shop can provide interesting insight into human nature. Situational things you would not encounter in less unique surroundings. In a recent case my vantage point in Dean's Automotive was a padded vinyl chair selected for its position to capture sunshine pouring through the floor-to-ceiling window. I couldn't miss the portly young woman who busted through the front swinging glass door to ask the guy working the customer counter how her two peanut machines were doing.

"Do you still want to keep them by the front desk?" she said.

"Sure. They're doing great," he replied.

The woman smiled and walked out the door to where her late model Ford sedan was parked to retrieve two 1-gallon plastic jars of nuts from the back seat. Looking more serious now, she came back in, went over to one of the old-fashioned, glass-bowl peanut machines at the back wall of the lobby, unlocked it and removed a fist-full of quarters with a few loose peanuts. After repeating the ritual with the second machine, she walked over and handed an empty plastic filler jar to the man managing the counter who had been watching her intently. He pretended to be surprised but my read was he was embarrassed about the surety at which she approached him.

As if on cue, once the front desk exchange was completed, a tall, lanky mechanic came in from the high bay garage adjacent to the lobby, wiping his hands on a faded red rag. She turned at him to smile before handing over the other empty jar. "Thanks." he said. As if sensing a need to explain, he continued, "They work great to store my fish eggs in."

I had noticed the big mechanic earlier that morning. He drove into the front parking lot towing a jet boat with at least two dozen rods lined up across the transom. When he came in the door, I asked, "Think you have enough rods?"

With a harrumph, he said, "You ought to see my garage!"

The peanut woman stuck around to make sure both coin mechanisms worked correctly and to gossip about a wreck she saw in front of the shop earlier in the week. After she collected her equipment and drove off, I couldn't help wonder about motivation behind what appeared to be at best a break-even business. Until then, I'd never thought about the ubiquitous peanut and gumball machines stationed at commercial outlets such as this auto shop. Was it a franchise? How did one go about finding a slot in the business of servicing peanut machines? And what was the value of the business for this proprietress. Was it for the handful of quarters or for attention received from appreciative mechanics that coveted her extra plastic jars to store fish bait in? No matter. The enterprise appeared sustainable; few moving parts to break down, the peanuts were eventually consumed, and the filler jars were recycled to a good cause.

Closet Bait Fisherman

My addiction to bait fishing traces back to the day Mr. Stanley was found stone-cold dead along the bank of the Umatilla River. The start to his day was innocent enough. I greeted him at the front doorstep with an order of two dozen red wrigglers. We argued briefly when he offered up a quarter, but only because I thought the deal was a quarter per dozen. From my perspective, the fact that his ticker gave out barely mitigated for the fact I had been wronged. So much for repeat business.

That day was one hint that I had been raised on the wrong side of the crick. As further evidence of a dark side to my angling persona, my teen years were spent drifting worms under root wads and through lazy holes of spring-fed creeks that emerged from the Blue Mountain foothills. My arsenal was expanded to include Band-Aid boxes stuffed with grasshoppers and Pautzke's "Balls O' Fire" salmon eggs ("soft but satisfying") that I stored in my cheek like a baseball player holds chew. It was those early experiences with bait that taught me how to read the water and bring trout to the creel.

Hunting for nightcrawlers the night before opening day of trout season became an annual ritual. I crawled on my hands and knees in the dark looking for subtle movement or the reflection of moonlight on their slime layer. Then, there was the grab. I hung on with perfect tension so they couldn't slip out of my grasp, pulling gently yet surely so as to not break them in half. Bait-hunting adventures taught me about patience, stealth and habitat association. These skills are equally applicable to fishing.

Such poignant memories are the main reason why I don't support the notion that bait fishing is the lowest form of angling. Simply stated, it's not fair that bait is out of vogue when it can provide a good experience. Black lights, paisley shirts and water pipes also come to mind in this regard.

Another reason I haven't given up fishing with bait is the overwhelming logic against artificial lure-only rules. First and foremost, using bait is natural. Second, catching fish with bait is not really cheating unless it is against sport fishing regulations. It's also difficult to buy the notion that bait fishing ain't ethical. It's a well-known fact that even the best lawyers struggle to articulate the difference between what is legal and what is ethical. The real issue should be about harvest, not that jurisprudence should result in angling impotence. After all, isn't one purpose of fishing to catch fish?

Whether having to do with dirty fingernails or different gear, bait fishermen are routinely segregated on western waterways. How else can you explain "artificial lure only" locales? I'm surprised that there has been no counter movement towards "bait-fishing-only" events. Participants could be enclosed like smokers at an airport, enabling them to destroy the resource and offend each other in a carefully controlled manner.

Okay. Maybe that example was a little over-the-top. However, it's not far from what many anglers believe, i.e., that there is no lower life form than one who puts bait on a hook. Could it be that these purists have their stocking foot waders on a little too tight? Why is there such a tendency to be fur- and feather-centric about what we put it front of fish? I'm thinking that color-coordinated outfits from Orvis are merely a guise, a cover for past sins.

Before proceeding to rat out closet bait fishermen, I must confess that I don't feel good about my addiction. Some days the truth weighs so heavy on my conscience I wish I had embraced organized religion, paid penance and moved on. So, rather than spend the rest of my life confused about the hold that bait fishing had on me, I searched for solace in the classic literature. The rationale was to understand myself better in order to help others. Anything to prevent another Saturday afternoon at the local chapter of Bait-Fishers Anonymous.

A sojourn to the city library revealed that the poet Ralph Waldo Emerson had extended the use of bait in artful prose: "Beauty without grace is the hook without the bait." Admittedly, I read the passage three times and still could not figure out what the heck it meant.

Digging deeper into piscatorial archives, I found bait fishing firmly embedded in leather-bound books. For example, William Shakespeare wrote "Bait the hook well, this fish will bite." Izaak Walton, the father of fly fishing, thought so much of bait that he devoted several pages in *The Compleat Angler* describing "many sorts" of bait, as well as their care and specific use for catching trout and minnows. Henry David Thoreau wrote of taking eels "with a mess of worms strung on a thread." Even Papa Hemingway used a grasshopper or two in his day.

Although this search provided a huge stamp of approval for bait fishing, I cannot reinforce enough that we must have standards. If not, the sport of angling could deteriorate into a reckless quest for fame like so many professional athletes on steroids. Consequently, and given the tremendous pressure on performance for angling, I have developed a series of tests to determine if your fly fishing buddy has a weakness for bait. Trust me on this topic. It takes a criminal to catch a criminal.

The clues are not intuitive. For instance, it is not possible to ascertain if your buddy is a bait fisherman by the number of horses contained under the hood of his extended cab pickup truck, the span of his significant other's backside or the number of Styrofoam containers in a garage refrigerator. Instead, look for a half-empty box of Borax on a workbench, the pinkish stain of Pro-Cure on a cork rod handle or a jar of Smelly Jelly in the interior pocket of a fishing vest. Maybe you saw your pal digging for garden hackles when you jogged by one evening and he explained, "Just re-charging the compost pile. "

Give me a break. Who is fooling whom? I suppose he also signed up for Entomology 101 at the local junior college. Just remember that behind every Egg-Sucking Leech or Glo-Bug is a fly tier who knows something about the advantage of bait.

In the absence of physical clues, look for behavioral ones. For instance, your fishing buddy might sit stoic while others talk down bait-loving fishes such as catfish and sturgeon. You might note he is overly rude to bait casters when sharing the water (that is, exhibits reformed "baiter" syndrome). Do his eyes light up like magic when you share what a few drops of shrimp oil could do to a Prawn Fly? Or, does he bounce a bead-head nymph on the stream bottom under a strike indicator, a fancy name for what everyone knows is really a BOBBER. And we all know why bobbers were invented: revenge of the redneck.

A clincher is if you catch your buddy standing in the middle of a stream on a hot summer day when those dang trout refuse to rise, carefully extracting caddis fly larvae from their pebbly case, and placing them in a plastic vial. When challenged he will almost always answer that he was only studying their stage of development.

Sure, and you can drink all the Bud Light you want and you won't feel a thing. The truth is that your buddy was serious about threading the juicy, worm-like, high-calorie morsel half-way down the shank of a #12 Adams to see if hungry trout were sulking in the vicinity. Whether he is a nervous backslider or a first-time user, you may never be able to prove. The bottom line is bait fishing is one habit that is hard to break. If you don't believe it, just ask me.

BAD NET JOBS

WHY DOES NETTING a big fish always turn out to be time of great angst? I know I'm not alone in having my heart broken after leading a trophy-sized specimen to the net only to have it escape. A recent, particularly painful event involved my brother who I can't blame because he had never netted any kind of a fish before.

It was a Hanford Reach trip that involved several hours of trolling with unrealized anticipation before I hooked a large salmon. Adding to the challenge was strong current and a 20 mph wind. Only after several minutes of steady pumping and reeling did I manage to get the fish close to the boat. The debacle began when Daran made several confused jabs, trying to "trap" the virtually moribund fish by forcing the net frame over its head and body, in the process tangling my Kwikfish in the net mesh. Seeing that the plug was tightly clenched in the salmon's jaw, I lowered my rod tip, grabbed the net and leaned over the gunwale while attempting to twist the net frame under its head. Unfortunately, all the pulling and pushing worked the plug out and my derby winner was last observed drifting downstream and out of sight.

Then there was a McNary Dam steelhead that pulled a disappearing act at the net. The day started with a cool breeze ruffling the surface of the river and hazy skies that added up to perfect trolling conditions. My buddy Bob and I worked the north shore-line of McNary reservoir with Wiggle Warts. Suddenly, my rod tip jerked like it had a seizure. I grabbed it from the rod holder as my hi-vis line carved a big arc across the water's surface. Peel-ing out line was a big steelhead that did a back flip before taking off on a long run. Following much back-and-forth action, I eased a mint-bright 12-pound hatchery steelie towards the open net held in Bob's capable hands. Adrenaline racing, I set my rod down and looked over the side to admire my trophy being lifted into the boat. That's when things got controversial. There was nothing in the net. The steelhead had escaped into the fourth dimension.

Leroy and an elusive summer Chinook salmon come to mind next. After having two fish toss an orange Magnum Wiggle Wart at the boat I switched to a pink plug modified by attaching the rear treble-hook to a 3-bead swivel. "The next one will get hooked halfway to the gills!" I exclaimed.

The sun was barely up over the hill when my rod tip went down to a small salmon that I horsed in. Leroy made a swipe with the net as the salmon thrashed on tight line next to the boat, managing to scoop it up. Upon further examination, my secret weapon, the trailing treble hook, was snagged in the net mesh. Leroy hauled in the salmon, hanging free on the outside of the net, held only by its long sharp teeth.

There's more. Later that morning brought yet another defin-ing moment that trips with Leroy are famous for. Losing confi-dence in "pinkie," I switched to a silver Wiggle Wart with a fluo-rescent yellow bill. This turned out to be a good move because I immediately hooked a salmon. "We could be in a patch of biters," Leroy said. "Keep the trolling motor going while you fight your fish in case one wants my lure."

This one had shoulders. I played it carefully, keeping tight line during a series of brief runs. When the fish got close enough to see the Wart firmly embedded in the corner of its toothy jaw, I worked it toward the boat to test state of tiredness. It wasn't until then that Leroy reeled in to help with the net job.

Spurred on by our sudden movement, the salmon took off on another long run, this time electing to stay top water. "Let's try bringing it in on the next pass," I said, hoping to close the deal.

Leroy argued for pulling the salmon around to the starboard side of my boat. "There's not enough room for me to stand on the other side."

It didn't make sense to land the fish with the downrigger and steering wheel in the way, but I didn't feel like arguing so I took position behind Leroy and worked the salmon back to the boat again. By now, it was leaning off kilter and at the surface. Its dorsal fin stuck out of the water like a feeding shark as I led it towards the net with my trolling weight snugged up to the rod tip. What happened next was a blur. In the blink of an eye the salmon went from the frying pan to freedom. It dove under the boat and my Wart popped to the surface.

"You must be sx#x!!ing me," I yelled in disbelief.

"I didn't want to knock it off at the boat so I pulled the net back." Leroy replied.

"Did you even get the net in the water? All you had to do was put it under the fish when I led it in."

"Your net handle is too short. Why don't you get a bigger net?"

"I don't have a clue why you wanted to net the salmon with the downrigger in the way in the first place.

"Your boat is too small. The seats were in the way. I couldn't maneuver."

"I'll gladly pay for yoga training so that you might gain flexibility."

It could have gone on like that for hours but I already felt like an idiot for losing my third salmon of the day with at least 30 boats watching. "Let's just not talk about it. It was just one of those things. The salmon was obviously not ready for the net," I said.

We trolled in silence for the next hour. I hoped for one last chance. Leroy hoped for anything. Twice he jumped up when his rod tip twitched, only to return disappointed to his resting spot on the bow. "Must have been a piece of milfoil," he explained.

It was noon before we called it quits. The first and only small salmon floated in the cooler, blanched in an ice water soup, surrounded by beer cans and food wrappers. It wasn't until we had driven halfway home before Leroy remarked, "We usually talk about fishing on the ride back, but you don't want to talk about it since you lost three salmon and I don't have anything to talk about because I never hooked any."

He was right. Recounting all the lost fish would make me look like a fool. That said, the fact he spent 14 hours on the water without so much as a pull-down while I hooked four fish sucked even worse. I decided to save that fact for later.

Such controversial net jobs are not limited to actions of my fishing buddies. In fact, I've got a few stories to tell on myself. And for some reason, most of these experiences involved Archie. In one subpar performance, I snagged his landing net on a gunwale cleat as a large salmon was being led to the boat. I then managed several pitiful stabs at the salmon's backside before tangling the lead dropper weight in the net mesh. This novice move led to a highly compromised situation where the net frame could not be brought within 3 feet of the salmon unless it chose to do a loop-de-loop on slack line and swim into the net on its own volition. Luckily, that particular 38-pounder ended up in the boat.

That story can be contrasted to another incident where, in my mind, I made a great net job on an out-of-control fish. Archie recalls it as a disaster. While drifting roe for spring Chinook salmon from an anchored drift boat on the Yakima River, Archie hooked two salmon on successive casts from the inside position while I watched his technique. I cleanly netted his first fish on the bank side of our drift boat. Archie brought the second fish to the outside of the boat where it battled strong current, jumping wildly when I made a stab with the net. This is where great hand-eye coordination came into play. I followed the salmon's upward momentum, lofted it chest-high and batted it into the boat. Unfortunately, it crash-landed on top of an open tackle box. While Archie sorted out the mess, I moved to the favored side of the boat and cast towards a current seam I had been deprived of earlier.

Interesting situations are not limited to salmon and steelhead. For instance, Archie started off a walleye trip by instructing long-time fishing buddy Fred on proper use of a net. As explained by the master: "Head first not the tail. Lead it to the net. Hold the mesh in your hand and stay away from cleats. Don't go for it too early."

The first walleye of the day did not provide a test of Fred's netting prowess because it chewed off Archie's leader before it could be steered it into the net. "Man, that one gave me the shakes. It's been a long time since I felt like that," Archie shared.

Meanwhile, the big walleye floated on its side, just out of reach at the surface, spent from the brief struggle. Archie encouraged the bow-mount to move closer, but a gust of wind pushed us away as the walleye twisted sideways to disappear into a boil of current. Remembering how I screwed up a previous net job or two, I wondered if Archie blamed me for not netting the fat-bellied exotic. Not that I felt guilty for past sins, but if the water had been 20 degrees warmer, I would have dove in after it to prove my mettle.

Fred soon quit fishing to look at the bottom of the river with an underwater camera. Equally bored, I let my jig trail aimlessly behind the boat. Meanwhile, Archie stayed on task, doing the foxtrot on the bow mount foot pedal. His patience was rewarded with two suckers and another walleye. "Snagged. Dang." Archie noted, when the walleye came in sideways.

When Fred netted it, Archie said, "Nice job getting in front of the head."

Given the plethora of detailed reinforcement dished out, I couldn't help but wonder if Archie was trying to tell me something without stating the obvious. My 4-year old grandson could have netted that complacent walleye. There was no good reason to think that Fred needed coached after at least 800 fishing trips. I shook it off. Nobody wants to be thought of as a bad net man. After all, I know the difference.

Reaching down to pull the jig from the walleye's dorsal fin, I took a spine across the fat part of my ring finger. Medical alert! I stuck my finger in my mouth to restrict the rapid flow of blood now leaking onto my shirtsleeve and pants.

Not to fear for in my wallet was a Band-Aid saved for such an emergency. I unwrapped it one-handed while keeping pressure on the cut with my thumb. "Man, this Band-Aid is so old, it's stiff," I said.

For some reason, Fred and I became inspired to fish again. We cast alongside Archie for several minutes before Fred chuckled. "What's so funny?" I asked, wondering what struck the normally stoic Fred as humorous.

"How's your cut breathing?" he replied.

"What?"

"The piece of paper floating loose from your so-called Band-Aid had Breathe Right printed on it. Unless I am mistaken, you put a nasal strip on your cut finger."

No doubt, using a sleep aide to stem the flow of blood from a laceration put me into a different category of angler. So it goes, but more important and back to the topic of netting fish, what can be learned from this series of misadventures?

First, there are more variables to deal with than tiring a fish before a decision should be made to lead it towards a net. Factors such as size of the net frame, handle length and mesh material influence the speed and distance afforded of a fateful stab. Add to the mix strength of river current, direction of wind, angle of sunlight, and location of protruding boat parts (not limited to cleats, anchor lines and engine props). I must also mention that all big fish invariably make a move away from or under the boat if provided the opportunity. However, these variables pale relative to acts of stupidity that come into play with the human dimension—some aberrant behaviors illustrated by foibles I have witnessed and/or been guilty of.

In the end, the crime of losing a fish at the net is directly proportional to their size and your overall batting average. And if there is one thing I have learned from these debacles it's that your fishing partner might eventually forgive but he will never forget.

STILL SMOKIN'

WHENEVER I LOAD my vintage front-loading Outers with a batch of fish, I figure it is for the last time. The smoker is pretty much a goner. I have re-wired the heating element four times. The bottom tray is rusted out and patched with heavy-duty aluminum foil. The door is warped and won't close. A rich patina of a thousand smoking events encrusts the interior. So much that caramelized fish juice drips on each rack of filets.

My smoker is like an old crippled hunting dog that I don't have the heart to put to sleep. The most recent problem was the handle to the wood chip pan falling off. Wiring it in place came to mind but there was not enough good metal left to work with. I tried an old Boy Scout aluminum frying pan from the same era as replacement, but it wouldn't fit through the tiny front door flap of the smoker so I rely on an oven mitt and a pair of pliers to refill the old pan with wood chips.

Another problem is the carbonized layer of goo that attracts neighborhood dogs like cats drawn to catnip. They would roll in it if they could only figure out how. I've thought of giving the smoker a good soak in the bathtub but my wife doesn't like the idea of smelling like burnt fish for the rest of her life. That left pressure washing as an option with the assumption rinse water wouldn't contaminate local groundwater. Which reminds that disposal in the local landfill would put the smoker in the category of hazardous waste.

I could upgrade to something akin to the $600 temperature-controlled, automatic chip-feeding smoker that one of my fishing buddies bought. However, he recently had problems with the electronics quitting in the middle of the night and lost a whole batch of fish. I could buy a pile of smoked fish from the butcher for that kind of money. Not that I would.

There have been numerous hints tossed to family members that a new smoker would make a nice gift but they have not committed this need to memory. I often wonder how long it would take for them to know the difference. Conversation at holiday celebrations might go something like this:

"Hey, dad. What happened to that excellent smoked steelhead you used to bring?"

"That was when I had a smoker. The old one fell apart several years ago."

"Maybe you should get a new one. I especially liked the dry-brine version."

What they don't know is the dry-brine holiday recipe is constructed like rough carpentry. I don't measure ingredients and the recipe ain't on paper. What I do is cover a pile of steelhead filets with a liberal amount of brown sugar before adding a layer of salt. The exact ratio is eyeballed. After refrigerating overnight, the filets are smoked skin-side down for approximately 6 hours or until done. The work is refilling the wood chip pan every hour or two and juggling racks to ensure uniform cooking of the filets. It's the brown sugar glaze that keeps people begging for more.

I could be fantasizing about the whole state of affairs. Too much free time as a result of retirement can do that to a person. However, I sometimes feel that others take advantage of my good nature when it comes to supplying fish for holiday meals. As an example, e-mail instructions for a recent Thanksgiving dinner went something like this: "Bring one fresh-caught steelhead to grill and a smoked one for hors d'oeuvres."

My first thought to that holiday edict was, Okay, my sister makes a pie using canned pumpkin puree, my brother brings a salad of factory-bagged greens, my niece brings a bowl of Chex mix and the next-door neighbor shows up with a smile and a cheap bottle of wine. Contrast those contributions with me driving hundreds of miles to brave the wind, cold and rain for as many days as it takes to catch two steelhead and hanging around the house to shove wood chips into my tired old smoker until the fish is cooked to FDA ingestion standards.

Easy for them to say, but I would not be happy if my siblings no longer considered me as the designated family fisherman. The decrepit smoker will continue to function as is and I will happily chase steelhead to distant waters. We all have our cross to bear.

Yarn Gone Wild?

NEVER SLEEP NEXT TO a cat box. Don't drink beer, wine, Yagermeister and cheap whiskey all in the same night. Women resent being reminded they could afford to drop a few pounds. These are all things I learned the hard way. Yet what I didn't know until recently was that encouraging fishing yarns from a dedicated woman angler can also get you in trouble.

Things snuck up on me, mainly because I hadn't realized the extent of my friend Robin's interest in fishing until she greeted me in the office hallway with a wide-eyed grin. "I caught one this morning!"

"You mean a springer?" I replied, vaguely aware that she had been trying to catch a salmon.

"Yup, out of Chinaman's Hole," she bragged. "Marylee caught two."

Chinaman's Hole is a popular sport fishery in the lower Umatilla River that is widely known for combat fishing when the spring Chinook salmon run is at its peak. Being well familiar with the location, I had to hear more. "Let's get both of your stories at the same time," I said grabbing her by the elbow to lead into the bullpen office she shared with Marylee and two other co-workers.

Marylee looked up with a shy smile when I entered the room. Meanwhile, Robin continued to grin so wide that my cheeks began to hurt. She perched on the edge of her swivel chair and leaned forward to elaborate. "It was the first fish I ever caught. I tasted some spring Chinook last year and told myself I've got to get some of that."

"Let's hear the rest of the story," I prodded.

She started from the beginning. "We got up at 3 a.m. and arrived in the dark to find four people standing where we planned to start. You wade out from the shore below the falls."

Although I had fished Chinaman's Hole countless times, her description was too general, so I asked a few clarifying questions before we settled on a place along the east shore of the river known as "the willows."

"It was just barely light when I got the bite. It was one of the first fish."

I waited for her to provide more detail, such as how the bite felt, if the salmon took off on a long run, whether it jumped or if there was a wild moment with the landing net, but Robin was still. Meanwhile, her face stayed stuck on a major smile.

Although it appeared the story was over, I couldn't leave without hearing more facts. "What about you, Marylee?" I asked, hoping she had something more to share.

Robin primed the pump. "Marylee said oops! I think I have a bite too."

That's all the encouragement Marylee needed. "It was fun when it kept jumping out of the water," she said, her eyes sparkling.

Robin interjected, "It was a jack. Then, later Marylee caught another one."

"Really," I said. "How did that one fight?"

Marylee's face flushed as she briefly recounted the battle with her second salmon. "It was an adult. It ran across the pool, taking line out, zzzzzzzzzzzzzzzzzzzzzz."

I sensed Marylee was warming to the task, but was taken aback when out of the blue she blurted, "It was as good as sex!"

Wow, I thought, taking a deep breath to collect my thoughts. What an ending! But rather than do the smart thing and leave on a high note, I added, "I've heard guys allude to having a near sexual experience after catching a big fish, something to do with conquest and all that. But I've never heard a woman say it."

Marylee and Robin turned to smile at each other but didn't say a word. Suddenly I sensed I was a third wheel in the room, the odd man out. It was that ol' men from Mars and women from Venus thing. Still, I couldn't help wonder what Marylee had been referring to. And all this time I thought that women only wanted to be held. Maybe it was my imagination, but the dreamy look in her eyes appeared to resemble afterglow generated from a good romp in bed. Was it possible the Kinsey report didn't cover all the bases?

I turned to leave, ready to chalk the conversation up to another encounter with a woman where I came up clueless, but Robin fired back with more. Words flew out of her mouth like a sinner at a revival meeting as she replayed the post-battle part of her salmon adventure. "The guys told me to bleed the fish. I asked what was better, to cut the gills or tail. They said the tail. Then, they said I needed a picture. They told me to wade out and stand slightly downstream where the light was better (She stood up and raised her hands above her shoulder to demonstrate how she held the fish while moving into position for a photo-op). I reached for Marylee's slimy hand, missed it, fell back and dropped the fish in the water. It was still alive enough to swim away. I jumped in after it and got soaked. One of the guys got his net out and dipped around until he found it."

Then just like that, Robin reverted back to the same shit-eating grin she had when we first met in the hallway. It appeared the storytelling was finally over. I had been entertained, cajoled, placated and toyed with. But I wasn't smart enough to leave without a parting shot. "Tell me," I asked from the office doorway, "how did it feel to be the only two fisher babes in a group of 20 fishermen?"

Robin wasted no time responding, "One guy told us now we know what he feels like when he goes to Nordstrom's."

He might have come up with a different line if he knew what was really going on in their heads. As for me, the conversation proved, once again, that women have the moral advantage on guys. Even on the stream.

THE CAPTAIN

ᒳ

MY FISHING BUDDY Leroy is a devout believer in fishing plugs that have super power. The full extent of his obsession was not revealed, however, until I returned home after a long day on the river to find the answering machine flashing madly. Hitting the "play" button, I retrieved the first message, detecting a low, strained voice, much like a dying man. Once convinced the caller was neither a pervert nor a solicitor, I placed my left ear next to the machine.

The message went something like this: "Hey, uh Dennis, this is Leroy. You know that lucky plug of mine, the blue one with the golden belly that I caught those two coho on off the mouth of the Yakima River (He still won't tell me exactly where his secret coho hole is.) I can't find it. I've looked all over. It was the one I bought when we went on that fishing trip to the Walla Walla River. I would really like to find it because you know I broke the other one off on that last drift near the launch today. Maybe I left it in your rig. It could've fell out of my vest or something when I put my shirt in your truck. Think you could take a good look through your equipment? Maybe it fell down behind the back seat. I really would like to get that lucky plug back. I'd appreciate it if you would look for it. Give me a call if you find it. Thanks a lot. Uhhhhhhhhh, bye."

I felt sorry for Leroy, but not enough to go outside in the

frosty night air to ransack my truck. I deleted his message and went on to a second one. This one, also from Leroy, was an hour later. This time he was in complete control of his emotions. Speaking in a voice that was both confident and clear, he said, "Hey! Ignore that last message. I found my plug. Thanks a lot. Talk to you later."

Leroy catches more fish than me because of relentless pursuit. But, what that particular exchange proved was that he is no different than any other fisherman dependent on having a proven fish slayer in his tackle box. My challenge (or maybe my problem?) is that Leroy tends to dwell on his good fortune well beyond what is required to make a point. And, sometimes the experience is painful, like when he's got a good fishing story and I've got nothing to share in return.

One such a story involves a plug so lucky that it should have been insured with Lloyds of London. It was a two-tone silver and fluorescent yellow M2 flatfish, one of many variations on a theme of wobblers and wigglers designed to drive salmon mad. Worden's M2 flatfish has a long, cupped lip to make it dive deep and a row of gill-ports along the sides for visual appeal. It is purported by the manufacturer to have a 5-1 "skip beat" action where every five cycles of motion produces one erratic beat to give the appearance of vulnerability to predator fishes, such as salmon. The concept is far enough out on the cutting edge of understanding to almost make sense.

Leroy and I take an annual trip to Brewster, Washington, in quest of big, red-meated summer Chinook salmon that migrate upstream in the Columbia River in late June and July. These fish stack up off the mouth of the Okanogan River, 300 miles from the Pacific Ocean, waiting for fall rains to lower the water temperature. Until that atmospheric event, several hundred salmon mill around while a gauntlet of boat anglers attempt to entice them with the latest and greatest salmon-catching device. Leroy and I sign up for this 50-boat gig almost every year.

The implausible part of one such Brewster trip was that, after catching three salmon with the same lucky silver and yellow M2 flatfish, Leroy announced he was going to retire the plug. Heck, I've done the same with a golf ball after a hole-in-one. But, that's different. Golf balls don't hold their karma for more than a hole or two.

I couldn't let go of why anyone would retire a useful fish-catcher for perpetuity. After all, a lucky plug should not be retired. It should be used to catch fish until broken or lost. Because once a plug turns stale, you can never depend on it again. I know. I have a slew of plugs that refused to entice another fish after being stored in my tackle box overnight.

"What are you going to do, make a shrine of it?" I asked Leroy.

"Maybe," he replied.

"You could put it in a glass case and label it with something like 'Caught three summer Chinook off the Okanogan River, August 1, 2005.'"

"I might do that," he snorted.

After a long pause, (Pausing is an effective tension reliever Leroy employs whenever my quick wit crosses the line from clever to rude) he admitted to having a large collection of fishing gear retired from action. My interest perked. What deep, dark secret was about to be revealed? Inner persona sometimes surfaced when we hung out too long and tired of twisting conversation into anything having to do with fishing or sex.

Leroy reflected briefly before unloading, "I have a shoe box that I keep the corkie rig I used to catch my 20th steelhead of the year. In the same box is a Wiggle-Wart that I caught three coho with on the Yak, and then there's the lucky spinner I used to catch two steelhead out of the same hole. There's other stuff, too. I'm going to put this lucky flatfish in the same box," he said, with the pride of a flag-waving veteran.

Meanwhile, I shifted into my attention-deficit displacement mode, ransacking the tackle box for a proven fish killer. I lined up half a dozen lures before finally selecting a Creamcicle orange Magnum Wiggle Wart with teeth marks tattooed across its butt—a sure sign that it drove salmon wild. I attached the leader holding the big Wart to a downrigger clip and said a silent prayer as I cranked it down into the opaque green water of the Columbia River.

Less than an hour passed with no action before Leroy's rod tip buckled.

"Good for you!" I lied as he cranked on his salmon, consoling myself by humming a line from an obscure song by Commander Cody and the Lost Planet Airmen, "It should have been me ... "

While netting the salmon, it was impossible to avoid the sight of Leroy's lucky plug nested crosswise in its mouth. "When did you sneak that plug in? I thought you retired it."

"I put it on when you were fixing a sandwich," Leroy replied. "You were giving me such a bad time, plus I was hoping to fill my punch card."

One thing on my list of secret wishes is that Leroy would permanently stow the lucky M2 with other treasures from his great fishing moments. Something about getting pummeled on a regular basis. Unfortunately, he continued to bring it out selectively. And each time he tied the lucky M2 on the end of his line, another salmon was scored for the freezer. That's why I wasn't surprised when he included it in his arsenal for our next adventure at Brewster.

I must mention that we started this trip in completely different frames of mind. I was cautiously optimistic, hoping for a salmon or two, while Leroy bragged to all within earshot that he expected to limit out both days. Such bold rhetoric made me nervous but I kept silent because it is difficult to argue with a blowhard without sounding like a killjoy.

We no sooner left the wine country of southeastern Washington behind when Leroy fueled his attitude by rehashing a long string of fishing stories. It was yet another variation on the same theme, "I've had tremendous success with springers this year and not all at the same location. I've caught fish at every place I've fished and not gotten skunked once."

I nodded now and then to acknowledge without implying I was unduly impressed. I could have stroked his ego but I've never been good about using that approach to manage a conversation. There's a fine line between appropriate recognition and enabling encouragement.

After weighing the alternatives, and still without a clue how to shut off the fire hose of self-adulation, I remained on the low side of the conversation and let Leroy ramble. This trip was setting up to be an endurance test with several hours of trolling and a long ride home still in front of us.

I twisted in the passenger seat, stared out the window and tried to recall the last time I caught a salmon. In the absence of having a story of equal or greater magnitude to share, my only recourse was to wait out Leroy. It was a defensive ploy I periodically used to limit bragging by others. Admittedly, the technique is rarely effective when confronted with someone content to monopolize the conversation.

"I'm more interested in what those big summers will hit," I finally interjected when Leroy stopped talking to take swig of root beer. "Wonder if it will be herring, Kwikfish, or Wiggle-Warts that gets their attention this year? Or, did you bring another piece of gear that I never heard of just so I can spend the day netting your fish?"

Leroy grinned and assured me the secret to success was contained in his tackle box. "I have my lucky plug, a backup one like it, and a brand new one I want to try out. If the new one doesn't produce, then I'll go to the backup. The backup has already caught four salmon. I might not have to use my lucky plug."

"Why don't you go straight to the lucky plug since you already know it will catch fish? Why screw around with a substitute when you have the real McCoy?"

As a scientist during his day job, Leroy is used to developing hypotheses, testing and revising them to explain experimental data. So it was no surprise that he had already thought about all the possibilities.

"I don't want to snag it on the bottom and lose it if I can catch a fish on one of the others. Plus, if I catch a salmon on the newest plug, I'll have three proven fish catchers in my tackle box." (Emphasizing the word "three" to rub it in.)

Leaving the Brewster boat launch in high spirits, we motored upriver to the mouth of the Okanogan River. A light breeze provided perfect conditions for trolling. Steep rock slopes above the bank of the river glowed shades of magenta and orange as the afternoon sun sank towards the western horizon. Three other boats motored in slow circles across the mile-wide expanse of reservoir.

As promised, Leroy started with the newest plug. However, 2 hours of trolling later, he upgraded to the backup one. The reality of trolling in figure eight's without so much as a bump had brought him down from an early high. "All it takes is one salmon for a successful trip," he said, forgetting about the other seven fish he promised to deliver to friends back at work.

This time, I was the one taking a more positive view.

"One apiece would be nice," I said, well aware that his revised goal of one salmon did not involve me.

At the 3-hour mark and still without a strike, Leroy had no choice but go to his designated hitter. As he opened his tackle box, I couldn't help notice scotch tape affixed to the top of his lucky plug. Carefully scrawled in black ink was "The Captain." Leroy's face glowed like a proud papa when he peeled off the tape to tie the plug to his leader.

I try not to get hung up over detail but it was clear this particular plug had taken on a revered status. There was to be no shoebox shrine for this one. Somewhere in the background I could swear angels were singing. This plug was slated to catch fish until either it broke off or was mangled obsolete by the hooked jaw of a giant salmon.

Leroy cranked the lucky M2 down to 30-foot depth and we resumed blank stares across the wide expanse of Lake Pateros. Less than a minute passed before his rod tip went down, whereupon Leroy set the hook with a loud bellow and cranked down on the drag. In no time he brought the dim-witted salmon to the boat, wasting no time before screaming at me to get the net. I absorbed his frenetic behavior in amazement being one who tends to milk a fight due to not knowing when I might hook another fish.

The landing of this salmon stimulated a new round of discussion about the lucky M2's special qualities. One train of thought led me to wonder when fish-catching events cross over from calculated opportunity to pure-ass luck. In doing so, I began to argue with Leroy—something I should not do when my self-esteem is low. "Catching two salmon in a row with the same plug is not independent of the first salmon-catching event if you don't change plugs. There is no way of proving whether the second salmon was attracted to that plug or whether it struck randomly. It could have been the location, boat speed, depth of presentation or even the time of day. Alternatively, the fact that you hooked the salmon might be entirely due to the fact we finally crossed paths with a 'biter.'"

Leroy ignored the mindless babble. Having recently marked a salmon on his punch card made him the indisputable expert. Although plausible, my explanations could be considered unconstructive. Downers are not encouraged while fishing. That could be why Doubting Thomas was never invited back to the Sea of Galilee. All good salmon fishermen must continually seek answers to the question, "Why?" Relying on a random collection of plugs to catch small-brained fish is not helpful in that regard. And that's why the very thought of losing a lucky plug can make a fishing buddy whimper and whine.

Liver and Onions

IF THERE'S ONE THING I've learned about trolling for salmon it is that fighting the wind makes me frantic. As a result, I keep my boat on the trailer to cast for spring Chinook salmon from the bank when the Columbia River shows whitecaps. This resolve left a quarter-mile long stretch of shoreline near the Ringold fish hatchery as the only choice on a blustery morning in early May. Unfortunately, a dedicated line-up of plunkers crowded the willow-lined shoreline from the irrigation canal downstream to the fence line boundary. Further upstream a group of drifters took over the mouth of the hatchery creek plinking Spin-n-Glos and herring strips. Downstream of the creek were several more plunkers. I moved into the only available space to cast my go-to spinner: a silver-bladed, chartreuse body #6 Vibrax.

By 9 a.m., I needed a break so I wandered over to BS with a guy sitting on the tailgate of a truck. He had his back to the river, waders rolled down to his waist, as he stuffed down a handful of Doritos. "It's breakfast," he said, offering the open bag as I approached.

"Thanks," I replied, helping myself to a small handful. "You must have got up earlier than me if you're already into the Doritos."

"My girlfriend fixed liver and onions last night," he said. "I'm 46 years old and it's the first time I ever ate liver. I can't get the taste out of my mouth."

"You definitely need fried onions on the side if you want to get liver down," I replied.

"And bacon and mashed potatoes," he added.

As we talked, childhood memories surfaced. I couldn't help but keep the thought train going. "I was raised on liver but refuse to eat it now," I shared. "I used to cut it up into tiny pieces and work it into my potatoes to kill the taste."

"Women seem to like it," he said.

"I agree but I'm not sure why," I replied. "Seems like some people have a craving for things that leave an odd taste in your mouth: animal innards like liver and brain, wild duck, fried oysters. I lump them together as food groups to avoid. You can have it all."

"Amen, friend," he said. "Thanks for your support, but I need those chips back."

I returned to my wind-swept casting station on the wide cobble shoreline. My new comrade in spirit dangled his legs over the tailgate of his truck nursing the same bag of chips when I gave up on springers an hour later.

CASTING FOR VARMINTS

༰

"LINDA, YOUR DOG peed on the corner of the front porch again."

That's how my best friend Bill started off dinner conversation with his kid sister Linda on my first overnight visit to his family's ranch house on upper Wildhorse Creek. I was 14 years old and sweet on Linda Lou, as called by close friends and family members. Linda Lou gave Bill a dirty look while I wondered if it was my turn to say something relevant. But I kept still, being nervous about how to attack the plate-sized piece of chuck steak that Bill's mom had planted in front of me. My family fished. We didn't hunt game, and due to seven family members at the dinner table, our consumption of red meat was limited to rather small pieces surrounded by noodles or vegetables.

It had already been an eventful day for this small town boy. One that included blasting ground squirrels with Bill's new, bolt-action .22 caliber Winchester rifle and later learning how to drive with a clutch. That is, if going zero for seven counts as blasting squirrels and driving a pickup truck includes doing your best imitation of riding a bucking bronco. But all was well after I polished off the massive steak and Linda Lou smiled to reassure.

Why this day flashed into my mind four decades later while standing in line at a lumber store in Pendleton, Oregon, I could only guess. Maybe it was because of a recent update on Bill, who lived nearby. Perhaps it was the sight of a stray dog lifting his leg. Or maybe it had to do with what transpired in the store.

I would have been fishing for steelhead except the mercury read well below freezing and I don't like to wear gloves. It's about maintaining an effective tactile relationship with the river bottom. Instead, I sped along a narrow one-way street through downtown Pendleton making a Saturday morning journey to our cabin, 30 miles further up the Umatilla River valley. The steel gray winter sky melded into Blue Mountain foothills dusted with new snow. Cruel gusts of wind sent leaves cascading down from twisted locust that lined the street. I slowed to miss a fat yellow dog peeing on the edge of the buckled sidewalk and parked at the main entrance to the Tum-A-Lum Lumber Company.

The Tum-A-Lum reminds of days before warehouse hardware stores squeezed out the little guy. It's wedged next to a 100-foot tall grain elevator at the tired end of a cowboy town famous for a world-class rodeo and the phrase "Let 'er buck." A tattoo parlor, defunct donut shop and a $40 per night motel filled in the gaps between the lumber store and worn wood-frame homes built in the early 1900s. What sets the Tum-A-Lum apart from its bleak surrounding is a second story façade sporting a carving of an Indian chief in full headdress.

Peering through a large picture window smeared with road splash, I made out the neon-lit outline of a second chief image that loomed over inside customers. Four rows of parallel aisles led to the main counter. Metal shelves were loaded chest-high with boxes of nails, screws and other fasteners. Racks of hand tools and small power tools, open shelving lined with tubes of calk, glue, Spackle, paint, varnish and miscellaneous hardware completed the inventory. The main counter spanned half the service area with a small office adjoining.

Two saloon-style swinging doors led back to the warehouse where you could wander among open stacks of plywood, dimensional lumber, trim molding, bundles of insulation, sheetrock and metal siding. The smell of freshly milled lumber filled the dusty air. But what kept me coming back was the wood. Their No. 2 pine boards were tight knot, planed baby-butt smooth and finish-ready after a quick pass of 120-grit sandpaper. One did not have to pick through the entire stack to get a straight piece like at Lowes or Home Depot.

Half a dozen customers clad in winter weekend attire milled around the front counter. A young guy sporting a fresh crewcut and a down camo jacket was reviewing items against a sales receipt held by a clerk. Slouched in the center aisle, hands jammed in front pockets, was a burly black-bearded man working a wad of chew in his left cheek. What got my attention though was a guy waving his arms and chatting it up with no one in particular about a recent antelope hunt in Wyoming. His Carhartt jeans were clean and freshly pressed. Sewn on the shoulder of his bright blue Gortex jacket was a Bass Pro Shop patch. The logo on his red baseball cap said Alumaweld. He might as well as had "guide for hire" tattooed on his forehead.

Waiting for the line at the counter to dwindle, I scrutinized a set of jigged bone handle knives locked up under glass. When the front door bell went off to signify yet another customer entering, I grabbed a 5-pound box of 10d common box nails and moved to a standby position.

Meanwhile, the guide was still on a roll. He cocked back the bill of his baseball hat and shifted gears from the high plains of Wyoming to the azure waters of the Sea of Cortez. "You guys ever fish Mexico?"

The room went silent. But some people, it seems, need little encouragement. He continued as if nobody else had anything to match up. "I actually won a tournament there once. They have fish down there that fight like you wouldn't believe. Roosterfish and dorado. One dorado chased our baitfish from over 100 foot away. It ripped across the surface like a macho shark!"

I watched his eyes narrow to sweep across the front of the room—much like the image of a shark. There was no response. Nothing. No wows, no grunts, not even a raised eyebrow. I could only speculate that he had driven the small group to boredom by incessant yammering or they had heard it all before. In either case, maybe taking a hint or maybe not, he bid farewell to exit through the saloon-style side door.

The door had barely stopped swinging when the bearded guy in front of me slipped his right hand out of his pocket to slowly stroke his beard and casually remarked, "Hey, did you guys ever fish for ground squirrels?"

It was as if he had been standing in auditorium wings waiting for a cue. Again, the room was silent. Only the clerk looked up from the cash register to acknowledge. "We cut a long pole, made a noose at the end and went squirrel fishing in the pasture," the man began. "When a squirrel would pop its head out of its hole, we roped it in. We must have got 25 squirrels that way. It was some of the best fishing I ever had."

After delivering the grand finale, he stepped forward, slapped his hand on the counter and turned to walk out the front door. I moved up to put my nails on the counter with a sense of hallelujah. After carrying the burden of being a bad marksman since early puberty, it took a Saturday morning tale at the local lumber store to enlighten me on the alternative of casting for varmint squirrels. Would the clerk care to know?

THE WALL

WE NO SOONER STARTED down the highway before Leroy laid into me. "I don't understand why you like to fish Little Goose. You get bored when we troll for salmon or bobber-fish for steelhead. Yet, you'll stand around there waiting for a take-down for hours without complaining."

I smiled and didn't say a word. It was easier to let Leroy guess than explain my fascination for fishing a place locals called "The Wall." The truth was I found the venue entertaining. Fellow anglers were interesting and friendly. And, so far, I was lucky when it came to banging an occasional springer there. Plus, fishing involved little effort. All I had to do was stick my rod in a holder and wait for action. There was no boat to haul, no motor to mess with and no long hike to the river in the dark wondering if someone beat you to the spot. If I got bored, I could BS with a neighbor, wander the deck or daydream over the river. And, if I happened to be in outer space during a takedown, someone would attract my attention. Sure, it was not the sport of kings. But, it was a sporting event where you could be king for a day.

Our trip to Little Goose Dam started well before dawn. I arrived on schedule only to find Leroy still loading gear into the back seat of his long-bed, extended cab F-250. I couldn't help but think something was wrong. He was usually sitting behind the steering wheel with the motor running by the time I arrived.

I was reminded of the bossy e-mail message he sent the day before directing, "Be there at 4:30 a.m. sharp or else!"

'So why the lethargic attitude?" I asked, after parking my truck in his spare driveway.

"Don't feel good. Had one too many glasses of wine last night."

Sharing point of view with anyone within earshot was one of Leroy's strong suits. I bit my lip, feeling surprisingly good despite the early start. As it turned out, our disparate attitudes would carry through the day.

We headed east towards Highway 12 chasing a tangerine glow that slowly enveloped the horizon. Rather than enjoy the beautiful sunrise, Leroy complained about lack of sleep and the price of gas. I ignored him while chewing on an apple fritter. "You seem to forget that I offered to drive."

"The bed of your truck is too short. Don't like to break my rod down."

Following that terse exchange were long stretches of silence as we cruised past acres of hybrid poplars and expansive rows of wine grapes that stretched across rolling hills in both directions. Telephone poles provided the only vertical relief in an otherwise flat landscape. These things you notice when not engaged in conversation. The highway was clear of traffic except for an occasional farm truck we quickly passed.

It was an hour and a half from Leroy's back door stoop to Little Goose Dam, but familiarity with the road chewed up miles like it was a trip to the neighborhood grocery store. A dozen vehicles already waited at the south shore parking area. Leroy nosed his truck in line and we followed others single-file to the lower deck of the dam when the entrance control gate opened at 6 a.m.

I jumped out of the passenger seat before Leroy shoved the transmission in park in order to get a place at the rail. This move was critical. There were only twelve cast iron rod holders welded to the top rail of a cyclone fence overlooking the tailrace and we needed two of them to keep from standing at the rail holding our rods.

I secured rod holder #11 for Leroy and #12 for myself. Meanwhile, anglers piled out of vehicles to gobble up the remaining ones. A second group beelined upstream towards the powerhouse. They were veterans of The Wall having custom-welded rod-holders they clamped onto the steel top rail polished smooth from years of use.

The south concrete deck above the tailrace hummed like a Saturday market while anglers brought out coolers, set up lawn chairs and arranged their tackle. The year's large run of spring Chinook salmon had attracted a large crowd of veterans and rookies from surrounding towns. In addition to locals from Starbuck, Pomeroy, Ritzville and Washtucna, there were long-distance travelers who had put in 2 hours or more of road time from places as far away as Milton-Freewater and Spokane. The assemblage included clean-shaven farmers in white straw hats, old-timers in blue work coveralls, sleepy-eyed teenagers, and middle-aged guys in cutoff jeans and logo t-shirts. A few wives had even come along for the ride. For a small town boy like me, it was like coming home to a neighborhood picnic.

"Hey Larry. What do you say?"

"Not much. How are you doing?"

"Doing okay. Looking to catch a fish."

"Me too. I got one Tuesday, but it was wild. Had to release it."

And so on. It was, by all measures, a friendly gig. Regulars were intrigued by new faces and willing to share what they knew, a fraternity of sorts. Interaction among participants reminded me of a weekday "gangsome" at the golf club, the happy hour crowd at a local bar or the daily prayer meeting at the neighborhood church. Some folks were as dependable as a Maytag dryer, turning up every day or most every day if they could, until the season was over. Also in force were well-established behavior patterns. Newcomers like us were well advised to watch and wait before doing anything stupid.

I could sense that some regulars were checking us out. Would we join the larger group or show up just this once, never to show again? Only time would tell. But for the sake of making friends, I pretended I would be coming back.

Up and down the deck, anglers stretched their legs to lean against the rail. Others kept their eyes on their rod tips leaning forward from a sitting position in old-fashioned webbed or canvas lawn chairs. Farther down the tailrace, several plunkers set up station, hoping to intercept a salmon. The day was turning out to be a grand social occasion.

Little Goose Dam rises over 100 feet above the water surface 70 miles upstream of the confluence of the Snake and Columbia rivers. The spillway and powerhouse stretch nearly half a mile across and perpendicular to the river flow. The lower deck is shaded and cool except when sun climbs high in the sky. We fished from the south side of the river next to the navigation locks and in the shadow of a massive fish ladder that doubled back twice before rising 75 feet to lead adult salmon and steelhead past the project.

All eight of the spill gates on the north side of the river were dumping water. Their operation created a giant back-swirl that extended halfway across the river and pushed the main current back upstream along the face of the concrete wall. To keep lines from crossing (most rod-holders were about 10 feet apart), anglers used 36 to 48 ounces of lead on a dropper below short leaders. What I didn't find out until later in the season was that salmon had been piling up at the base of the dam for several days due to being confused by spill operations. Upstream passage for spring Chinook salmon had dropped off from 1000 to less than 100 salmon per day before anyone figured out what was going on. This behavior had been documented in the past, but "fixing" conditions responsible for passage delay of springers was not a priority of fisheries management agencies or the U.S Army Corps of Engineers.

The Wall is so-named because fishing involves lining up behind a waist-high cyclone fence and dropping gear down a 20-foot-high vertical concrete face to reach the water's surface. Once hooked, salmon are led along the deck, around a large concrete abutment and downstream to a set of steps that provide access to a riprap shoreline. Getting a salmon to swim that direction was the first challenge. Netting it while perched precariously on boulders made slick from constant wave action was the second.

On our only trip to Little Goose the year before, Leroy and I were lucky enough to get a spot next to a guy with a custom-built net having a 20-foot-long handle. He helped land our salmon from the inside corner of the concrete pillar where fish swam to rest out of the back swell. This netting method worked well for salmon that refused to be led downstream to the riprap. Rather than depend on the benevolence of a stranger, Leroy came prepared with a long-handled net that he built and tested over the winter.

I had a brand-new silver and blue, one-piece 6 1/2-foot Laminglass "stick" rated for 20- to 50-pound test line. Its black foam "easy grip" reel seat was matched to a Penn 320 GT reel. I felt like a little kid with a new pair of tennis shoes. On a previous trip to The Wall, I used my 10-foot long sturgeon rod but wasn't happy with the outcome. One salmon tapped on my cut-plug herring for several seconds before I became impatient and jerked it out of its mouth (apparently).

Learning from that experience, I let a second fish chew on fresh bait for exactly one minute before attempting to set the hook. Again, I came up empty. A third bite produced a solid take-down, but the salmon got off before I could get my rod out of the holder. This day would be different. I had a new rod and a fresh perspective.

A wave of excitement rolled through the crowd following an early hook-up. According to established code of conduct, all nearby anglers reeled up to let the lucky guy fight his fish. I peered over the rail to watch. Several seconds passed before I realized my line was in the way of a salmon moving fast along the wall. I grabbed my rod and reeled in like the rookie I was.

The first hour of the day was a jack-fest. Several salmon were hooked and landed, none over 4 pounds. Nonetheless, the steady action kept me pumped. In contrast, "Leroy's hangover had manifested into a full-blown depression. He worried the guy next to him would cross his line. He didn't like the action on his herring. He complained that I took the best rod holder. "I don't have a good feeling about this. I don't know why I came," he groused.

I ignored Leroy. One alternative was to ream him for trying to bring me down while I dealt with exactly what he was dealing with. However, it was too early in the day to go there. There were still options. I stretched and admired the scenery. I wandered down the line nodding good morning to others. I watched the tailrace current ebb and flow. I adjusted my drag. I lined up replacement herring.

Steve, in position #10, finally hooked up with a salmon. He wasted little time taking it around the corner of the concrete pillar and downstream to the riprap. "What happened," I said when he came back empty-handed.

"I released it," he said, matter-of-factly.

I watched out of the corner of my eye when Steve went to the back of his truck to put on fresh bait. He was the only one in the line-up using a double-hook rig. This set-up, combined with a 32 ounce lead dropper ball that swung wider in the fast current than the 48 ounce weights we had on, made Leroy nervous.

"He's right on my line," Leroy muttered under his breath.

Less than 15 minutes later, Steve hooked another jack. This one he let tire before hoisting it straight up the wall. He then pinned it to the concrete floor attempting to remove the hook, while it bled from the gills. His inept handling of the fish finally got to me. "That jack is as good as dead," I said, hoping that he would do the right thing and keep it.

Fat chance. Steve leaned over the wall and dumped the moribund jack back into the tailrace. Splooosh......... The fish disappeared into the turbulent flow. To be fair, Steve wasn't the only one practicing catch-and-release of unwanted fish. To my right, another guy reeled a jack up the wall. He did a better job of unhooking, but a worse job of releasing. When the jack struggled loose, it bounced off the concrete ledge by the rail and disappeared into swirling current. Soon to be crawdad bait.

Finally it was our turn for action. "Hey "Leroy, you're getting a bite," I said, observing something slightly more than the current pulling on his rod.

"I don't think so," he said, "My rod ain't even in the rod holder."

I looked again. The now-bouncing rod tip was mine. So much for staying on task, I thought. I pulled my rod out of the holder to set the hook but my line was slack. "Guess I missed it," I said to Leroy before feeling the pull of a small salmon.

My setup, 30-pound test main line and 10-pound leader for the lead ball, was designed to allow the lead ball to break free when a fish was hooked. But my leader held. The jack ran back-and-forth hampered by a 48-ounce lead ball. I leaned over the rail when it surfaced to check for an adipose fin. There wasn't one, signifying a hatchery fish, a "keeper," but I didn't want it. Given a one-fish limit, it was too early in the day to quit with one small salmon. So, I let the jack swim around in a circle, hoping for a volitional release. I didn't want to bring it up the wall and was too lazy to walk it down to the rip rap, so I jerked to shake it off. Unfortunately, both leaders snapped. My lead ball joined a large collection at the base of the wall and the jack swam off with my lucky Spin-N-Glo firmly attached to its snout.

A pattern emerged as salmon were hooked up and down the line. Jacks came quickly to the surface while larger adults stayed down deep. Meanwhile Steve continued to have the hot rod. He hooked another salmon after his bait had been in the water less than 10 minutes. I had eyed him packing the open body cavity of a small cut-plug herring with brown paste. This finding led me to soak my next bait in herring oil to add scent.

Steve kept his third salmon of the day with some remorse. Leroy speculated he felt guilty after killing the jack. We later found that Steve caught a 23-pounder the day before. This may have been a factor in his plan to grade out small ones.

Meanwhile, Leroy complained about bad luck. So much so that Steve shared a secret. "All the fish are caught between 21- and 24-foot depth."

Leroy was an instant convert. He dropped his herring down one short pull at a time counting out loud enough for me to hear over the roar of spilling water, "1, 2, 3, 4, 5, 6, 7, 8, 9, 10, 11, 12, 13, 14, 15, 16, 17, 18, 19, 20, 21, 22."

Being a non-believer of other's fishing theories, I stayed with my method of lowering the lead ball to the bottom and bringing it up four or five cranks depending on my mood. I repositioned my Spin-N-Glo when I got bored or when I didn't like how the herring swung in the current. Given the wide assortment of gear used by others, hooking a salmon appeared to be as much a random act of faith as skill.

I checked my watch when the sun eked over the powerhouse to envelop the deck like a spotlight on a stage. A constant cool breeze swirled up from the water's surface circulating the smell of musty concrete and fish bait.

I reeled in when someone at the top of the fence yelled, "Big fish on!" A buck-toothed guy in a flannel shirt worked quickly downstream through the line-up of anglers. He had on a large salmon that peeled out line and jumped wildly in the froth a stone's throw from the wall. The salmon refused to follow downstream. Instead, it moved towards the dam making a series of slashing runs along the wall and displacing the last group of anglers debating whether to reel up. I grabbed Leroy's long-handled net and followed the guy to the corner. "Are you sure your drag is tight enough," I said, when the salmon ran upstream towards the fish ladder entrance.

"It's really pulling hard," he replied, demonstrating by rocking back on his heels and holding his rod tip high. The fish responded by taking out more line. I sensed the source of his problem. The lightweight Eagle Claw fiberglass rod and a small level-wind reel were undermatched. Everyone else had short, beefy rods built to handle a big salmon, heavy current and the added weight of the lead ball. Tuna rods of the Ugly Stick variety were most common.

"Pump and reel," I encouraged.

The guy made no progress on a too-loose drag. By now the entire lineup of anglers had their baits out of the water and were out of patience. Feeling the peer pressure, he reeled frantically while I stood by his side with Leroy's custom net in my right hand. As the salmon flopped and twisted on top of the water, someone yelled, "Bring it upstream!"

I leaned over the rail hoping for a chance at the struggling salmon, but it dove and swam out of reach further down the wall. "It's snagged on the gill plate," someone else yelled, noting a white patch on the side of its head where a hook had worked a hole the size of a dime.

That's when the unwritten code of The Wall prevailed. One of the regulars leaned over the rail, grabbed the guy's line and broke off the salmon. You are only allowed so much time for incompetence. We all raced to get gear back in the water while the now ignored, disgruntled angler shuffled back to his place at the top of the fence.

Meanwhile, Leroy remained in a funk. I offered a Sobe.

"Not now."

I offered a fritter.

"Not hungry."

Despite being influenced by negative karma, Leroy's rod tip went down. A good-sized salmon, maybe 12 pounds, had grabbed his herring. I reeled in to help land it, but Steve grabbed my arm and told me to keep my rod in the water. "I'll take care of your fishing buddy."

I mulled the consequences for a split second before dropping my line back down. Steve seemed to know what he was doing and I wanted a fish of my own. It wasn't like I deserted Leroy. He appeared to be in capable hands. The end result was that I stayed put.

Steve grabbed a short-handled net leaving me to watch my rod tip hoping for a patch of biters. When I turned my attention away from my rod tip, Leroy was standing in position on the downstream side of the concrete pillar, fighting his salmon, Steve alongside with the net. Five minutes later, Leroy hadn't gained control to move downstream to the riprap. I noticed he looked anxious but he always looked anxious when fighting a fish so I focused on my rod tip.

About that time Steve walked back to retrieve Leroy's long-handled net. Noticing my inquisitive look, he said, "He wants to land his fish with this one in the corner pocket."

I could argue that Steve had the net job under control but the truth was I had more interest in catching a salmon than Leroy's plight so I stayed put. Unfortunately, the next time I looked up, Leroy was walking back empty-handed. "What happened?" I asked.

"I couldn't get it around the corner and I couldn't hold it any more. It broke off. I should have tried to land it with my long-handled net. The current was too strong to get it around the corner. I'm not blaming anyone. Steve tried to help. It's not his fault. He's a nice guy. I can't believe that I was so stupid."

"Don't beat yourself up," I said. "I would have come down there but I figured once you got the salmon to the corner, you would take it down to the riprap and land it with no problem. That's how it worked last year."

"The current is too strong. They won't go around the corner."

My guilt was building. I should have helped out. "It's early," I offered. We have time to get another fish."

"That was my chance," Leroy said. "If only I could have land-ed it with my big net."

It didn't improve the situation when I hooked the next fish. To his credit, Leroy didn't hold a grudge. He netted my salmon in the downstream corner of the wall where he wanted to land his. Although the lead hook of my mooching rig had pulled free, the trailing hook was buried deep in the salmon's isthmus.

I tagged the 10-pound hatchery hen and put my rod away. While Leroy fished, I killed time eating snacks, alternating swigs of Sobe and Guinness, rigging up Spin-N-Glos and making notes in my journal. Meanwhile, Leroy stood by his rod, shoulders slumped and with a glum look.

I took my salmon to the cleaning station before wandering up the line to BS with other anglers. That when I met Dave, one of the regulars. Dave showed off all his gear, including a collection of rainbow-colored spinner blades that he used to catch steel-head in the fall. "Caught two 20-pounders last year," he bragged.

When I asked about the 22-pull theory for springers, he snorted, "Shit, a few years back, it was 6 1/2 pulls to get to where the fish were."

I made myself useful by netting several salmon with Leroy's long-handled net. One fish was artfully retrieved on the outside of the bag with the trailing hook tangled in the mesh. I also fol-lowed anglers downstream to the riprap to observe the proper technique for getting salmon around the concrete pier. It turned out that two people were required. A helper held the angler's line away from the abrasive corner of the pier, stretching out as far as they could from the downstream edge, while the angler held his rod perpendicular to the walkway. Once the salmon tired, and if well hooked, it was maneuvered past the pier and down the walkway. Unfortunately, this newfound knowledge was acquired too late to help Leroy.

A bell rang up the line for Woody, the 86-year-old local farmer who was a crowd favorite. Woody grabbed his rod and slowly worked the salmon downstream while his buddies cheered. One angler bragged to me after Woody passed, "We take care of him."

When no one followed Woody down the wall, I thought, Yup, you take great care of him as long as he remains in the general vicinity. Still playing Good Samaritan, I left my post to net Woody's jack by the riprap, hoping to be fishing when I was his age.

I migrated back to the line-up to find a morose Leroy. You would have thought his dog just died. Thankfully, he got a second chance at a fish. This one was given my undivided attention. "Do you want to keep it," I asked when his jack surfaced.

"Yes." Leroy said, with bated breath, as he moved cautiously down the fence line towards the concrete pillar. I positioned with a tight grip on his long-handled dip net while he motioned to the inside corner for a better angle. Unfortunately, the net was not wet when Leroy said, matter-of-factly, "It's off."

It was almost as if he expected to lose it. Back at the truck, I cracked another Guinness and waited to see what else the day would bring. Leroy was now in the darkest of moods. Losing the jack had only polished the bad experience with the first salmon. Resting his elbow on the rail, he said, "This day is the worst." After spending the morning propping him up, I was worn out. Things had progressed to where all I had energy for was to wait him out. Mercifully, we called it quits at noon and headed to the Lyons Ferry Marina where Leroy's mood improved when I picked up the tab for his bacon burger. By the time we reached home, he managed a tired smile. It seems time heals all wounds.

———————— ↳ ————————

I waited a full week before heading back to Little Goose Dam for a season finale. Leroy declined to come along, explaining, "I need more time to recover."

There were only four anglers on the lower deck when I arrived. My new friend Dave was at the #3 spot wearing a Miller-Lite t-shirt and baggy blue shorts that exposed an artificial leg. A slender brunette in her early 40s was at position #10 (where I wanted to fish). She was what some might call "easy on the eyes." Fishing next to her was a tall guy with a full mop of brown curls, but they didn't appear attached. The entourage also included two kids, maybe 4 and 12 years old, and a plump woman in a lawn chair smoking a cigarette. Woody was also there. He sat on the tailgate of his truck further up the deck. I parked next to Dave's late-model Dodge truck and put my rod in holder #8.

Dave recognized me from the week before. "That's not the truck you came in last time. You must have come up in your buddy's truck before," he said.

"Where did everyone go?" I replied, trying not to stare at the source of his limp.

"They got tired of catching jacks and went home. I released three jacks this morning. I only had five herring left so I used shrimp. If I catch another salmon, I'm going to keep it."

I quickly attached a cut-plug herring to a green and silver Spin-N-Glo and dropped the rig into the powerful swirl. My rod tip bounced as the herring twisted and turned in the swift current. A slight breeze moved scattered clouds upriver. Across the river, rounded hills appeared like muffins browning in a pan.

Gulls worked the tailrace for disoriented smolts. Only three spill gates were open but the upstream swirl near the wall was still intense.

I hung over the cyclone fence while Dave carried on an animated conversation with the plump smoker. Their relationship had progressed to where she was out of her chair and leaning close enough to count the stubble on his chin. That's when Woody's bell went off to signify a strike. Rising to his feet, he struggled to get the rod out of the holder. Familiar with senior citizen moments, I left my station to assist. "Want to bring it up the wall?" I asked, adjusting the drag on his reel.

"We can't do that any more," he replied.

Woody then handed off his rod to me, apparently so that I would work the salmon around the corner of the concrete pillar, which I did, but he looked befuddled when I handed the rod back. I regretted not finishing the job because the hook pulled out of the salmon's mouth before he got halfway down the catwalk. Evidently I had not learned how to "take care of him" as per his regular buddies.

Things weren't exactly red hot so I changed venues by moving upstream towards the fish ladder entrance where current slowed. This move involved bolting down the $19.95 rod holder I bought at the general store in nearby Starbuck. Having the apparatus moved me up a notch in the hierarchy of The Wall. After tying on a new Spin-N-Glo baited with green-label herring, I slipped on a large corkie above the swivel to gage line swing and dropped my rig down the concrete face. The herring flashed and twisted perfectly in a tight spin. I felt positive about my chances.

When Woody and the curly headed guy pulled up their gear and left, I was left alone at the upper end. There was nothing to do but crack a Guinness and watch my line sweep slowly back-and-forth like a metronome in the strong current. As if by design, the rod tip bowed ensuing a series of sharp taps. I picked up the rod to feel the pull of a fish, but before I could reel up tight to set the hook, it was off.

Meanwhile, Dave hooked his fourth jack of the day. "It was only seven pulls down," he yelled.

Rather than lead the jack around the corner and downstream to the riprap as was standard protocol, Dave reeled it straight up the wall after noticing it was hooked deep in the eye socket. With little fan fare, he clubbed the flopping salmon with a tire iron and tossed it in a large white cooler. My expectations ramped up as Dave kept the two women entertained with fishing exploits. About this time, the brunette shared it was her birthday. Dave wasted no time following the announcement with an invitation to dinner and directions to his house. "We'll cook up this salmon. There's plenty for all of us."

The merriment was too much for me to ignore so I started across the parking lot to join in, but before I got halfway there, my rod tip began to twitch violently. Sprinting to the fence, I picked up my rod to feel what I thought was a decent-sized salmon, but was fooled by the extra weight of a 3 pound lead ball. When the jack rolled on its side, Dave helped me hand-line it up the wall. The hook set was deep in the jaw leaving something said for letting a fish hook itself.

Birthday girl moved quickly to my side to watch. Cheeks flushed red with excitement, she followed me to my truck while I put the jack on ice. "Is that a Michelob you're drinking," she asked, as I cracked a victory beer.

I may be naive but I know when a salmon groupie hints for a free beer. Plus everyone should know the difference between certain brands so I gave her my last Guinness. It was the least I could do after Dave gave her a fairly new level-wind reel he claimed was superfluous to his needs.

After we drained our beers, the women loaded their gear and kids in the Expedition. Before driving off, birthday girl offered Dave and I a goodbye hug. We took her up on it.

Dave and I discussed the series of events that preceded their departure while we stood side-side at the cleaning station. "She spent the last half hour following either you or me around saying it was her birthday and talking about how bad she wanted to catch a salmon," I said. "It was a good thing I ran out of beer or I might have given her a fish. In which case, I would still be fishing."

"I was thinking the same thing," Dave replied, as he hosed blood, slime and loose scales down the sink. "We're too much alike."

He rattled off his phone number and invited me to stop by "any time" I was in Walla Walla, leaving with, "There is always Bud Light in the refrigerator on the back porch."

While driving home I couldn't help but reflect on notable differences between fishing at The Wall and my recent trip for redside rainbow on the Deschutes River. Fly fishers on the Deschutes wore designer hats and $80 UV–protection shirts. Anglers fishing The Wall wore foam-mesh baseball hats and sleeveless T-shirts. Personal distance on the Deschutes is typically measured in tens of yards rather than feet. Some anglers ignore when you pass by. In comparison, anglers at The Wall want to know your name and where you are from. They share homemade cookies with anyone within shouting distance. They give advice to those who struggle. They want everyone to have a good time. They invite strangers home for fish dinner or a beer. Some even give hugs. I have no problem propping up a fishing buddy who suffers from mild depression for that kind of venue.

Nights on a Boat

Why sleep on the bottom of a boat when you could camp out in a tent, stay in a nearby motel room or sleep soundly in your own bed? I guess it depends on your sense of adventure, but in my case such trips usually start with the idea of saving a little money or not having to wrestle other boaters for a turn at the launch in the dark. One thing's for sure, every night-on-the-boat trip has led to a new and different experience, not to mention fresh insight into human behavior.

Conflict on the White Salmon River

The first time I slept in a boat to gain advantage over salmon almost led to fisticuffs. It started peaceably when my friend Dick and I left the Hood River marina in the dark to motor slowly across the Columbia River, our route aided by a single street-light on the north shore, intermittent headlamps from cars, and a full moon that shone a slanted beam across the white-capped surface like a lighthouse beacon.

We approached the mouth of the White Salmon River with plans to fish lighted plugs under the narrow-span Highway 24 bridge. Unfortunately, the idea, while inspired, was not original. Once our eyes adjusted to the dark, we detected a boat anchored directly under the bridge and another one tied off to a rope that hung from the adjoining railroad trestle. Upstream was a flotilla of steelhead anglers in float tubes. Their neon-tipped rods waved back-and-forth like Chinese lanterns in a New Years parade. Our attempts to anchor between two boats while buffeted by a strong west wind were rebuked while being advised to fish elsewhere unless we were looking for a fistfight. After this violation of personal distance, we moved upstream to more open territory.

Things settled down around midnight so we opted to anchor for a night under the stars rather than search for a cheap motel. Dick wedged his 6-foot frame behind the steering wheel, feet draped over the ice chest. I sprawled across the bow, supported by a life jacket and spare battery. The moon moved slowly across a star-filled sky. Its bright glow passed through the struts of the railroad bridge before disappearing, mercifully, behind the tree-studded horizon around 3 a.m.

My feeble attempts at sleep were interrupted by the constant clang of freight trains parading by. Seemed I had forgotten what happens when you try to sleep under a scenario that invites disturbance. I woke up tired, stiff and sore when the alarm on Dick's wristwatch went off at 4 a.m., but I wake like that at home so it was nothing new.

We crept out to the main river channel in pre-dawn black to a brisk breeze blowing directly upriver. Red and green bow lights from two other boats bobbed offshore in the chop. When the depth finder did not suggest anything special about the river bottom, we lined up with the downstream edge of the bridge and a point 200 feet offshore. A steady migration of running lights from the Hood River launch signaled the arrival of more anglers.

Dick landed a bright 22-pound Chinook salmon hooked on a purple-and-white crippled herring jig before the sun rose over the gorge. It was a docile fish that swam obediently to the boat where it was quickly netted. Sometimes a salmon does not sense it has been hooked until it's too late. Meanwhile, wind surfers cavorted on 4-foot waves outside the cluster of anchored boats while salmon jumped alongside like trained dolphins.

We traded morning naps to keep one jig in the water at all times. It wasn't until noon before I hooked a hefty 26-pounder that made several strong runs before responding to tight drag. Whether from lack of sleep or nervous anticipation, my legs shook until well after it was safely in the net. Dick hooked one more salmon but it broke off after getting tangled in another boat's anchor line. To eliminate further altercation with adjoining anglers, we packed up our gear to make the long drive home.

Head Banger off the Okanogan River

Leroy and I anchored in a shallow patch of milfoil adjacent to a gentle sloping gravel shoreline. The evening sky was lit up by a full moon having reddish glow due to smoke from forest fires. A light breeze kept the aft end of my boat pointing towards the Big Dipper. It was an idyllic scene largely wasted on two anglers worn out from an afternoon of trolling that yielded but one salmon for the box. I spread my sleeping bag on the padded bench seat, made an unsatisfactory pillow from a balled-up t-shirt and rested my head next to the auxiliary gas tank. Leroy laid his sleeping bag on the bottom of the boat between the bench seat and the live well, using two life jackets for padding.

While I lay on my back waiting for the magic of sleep to overtake my restless mind, Leroy rooted as if to make a nest. Sometime later, after a super-spinning holographic-inspired flasher from a rod leaning against the transom began to twirl and bang against the top of the main motor, I got up to re-arrange gear.

Through it all, Leroy lay still, either faking it or with a different REM pattern. I eventually drifted off to sleep only to be awakened by Leroy standing over me to dump out a small ice chest. "It was sloshing around by my head," he said.

I grunted dissatisfaction at the interruption before drifting off to another brief tryst with Morpheus. However, this nap was also short-lived as the wind began to gust. While my head rocked and banged against the hull, I slept in fits and starts, dehydrated from a long afternoon in the sun.

There's something magical about a full-moon night and sleeping in the open. While an awesome experience, a full moon confuses the pineal gland to sense you left the hallway light on. During one insomniac moment, I sat up to admire a brilliant cascade of stars. Through it all, Leroy snored like a chain saw. That's the way it works. One person lies awake while the other guy sleeps soundly. When you finally nod off, the other guy lays awake thinking that you are getting all the z's.

The sound of aluminum scraping on gravel eventually penetrated the dawn. It seemed some time during the night the wind shifted to lift the bow anchor off the bottom and pin us against the shore. Leroy rustled awake at the sound to groan, but I ignored him because my head throbbed and I was sticky from sweat. "It's 4:30," he announced.

The first thing that came to mind was, *"Who gives a shix@!?"* but I remained quiet because talking would make my head hurt even more than it already did.

Leroy rolled up his sleeping bag. I turned over and kept my eyes closed, grunting in reply only after he asked if I had plans to get up. Later in the day, he commended me for not complaining, "Like you always do."

"My head hurt too much to talk," I explained. "Just because

someone doesn't complain does not mean they feel okay."

"I never thought about that," he said.

"That's because you always complain when you aren't happy." I replied. "You figure everyone else acts the same way."

"Oh" was the best he could come up with, but I think he got the point.

High and Dry at Wanapum Dam

It was the afternoon of the day before my 53rd birthday when I met my son-in-law at the Wanapum Dam boat launch. Hoping to bang a few late-run fall Chinook salmon, we pulled sardine-wrapped Kwikfish on lead ball droppers near the railroad bridge until dusk. The plan was to anchor up and sleep downstream of a section of steep basalt cliffs that framed the west shoreline. Unfortunately, our preferred location was exposed to steady 30 mph winds blowing upstream through Sentinel Gap. So we motored to the lee side of an adjacent rock formation to drop anchor for the night.

I should have known better but I didn't. The Columbia River immediately downstream of Wanapum Dam is subject to power-peaking operations that raise and lower the river surface several feet in a matter of a few hours. The end result of the oversight was waking around 2 a.m. feeling upside down. While Will and I slept soundly on the bottom of the boat, the river level had dropped, leaving the bow of my 17-foot Sylvan high, dry and tilted 30 degrees towards the sky. The main motor shaft wedged in a rock crevice to provide an effective fulcrum. I woke up Will, who slept soundly in a more comfortable upslope position, and, with the aid of gravity, we dislodged the motor and slid the boat back into the water. This time we anchored up in deep water.

the barbless HOOK

More Thunder and Lightning at Brewster

Twice in two years, the evening bite for summer Chinook salmon off the mouth of the Okanogan River was interrupted by a summer thunderstorm. The first time, we fished out of Leroy's open boat. He opted to anchor near the Brewster launch well before sunset, concerned that lightning might strike the boat. In contrast, I had hoped to enjoy the spectacular display of Thor's power, comfortable with lightning bolts 20 miles or more away to the north. Seems everyone has a different comfort margin.

Bob and I didn't have a choice but to quit fishing a year later when the interval between thunder peals and lighting strikes closed to 10 seconds. Disregarding the evening bite, we left open water and whitecaps for the Brewster City Park as the storm hit with full force. Luckily, (and unlike a similar experience with Leroy), I had the top up on my 20-foot Hewescraft to provide shelter from the pelting rain. After we found a place to anchor, I lay lengthwise on the bottom of the boat with my head under the top and a small blue tarp spread over my legs. Bob made all 5 ft 8 inches of himself cozy lying crosswise under the console. Unfortunately, I neglected to bring along side curtains, so water dripped on his head until the storm passed and skies cleared. With the aft end of my boat facing southwest, I traced the moon's arc across the star-lit heaven before it dropped beneath the distant ridge just before sunrise.

Drano Lake Folly

As to where to fish for summer steelhead in Drano Lake, prime locations are no more of a secret than a celebrity's tabloid mistress. Most anglers anchor up to bobber fish in the old river channel that starts in the northwest corner of the drowned mouth of the Little White Salmon River, runs along the north-

100

west shoreline and out to the Columbia River. What's attractive to steelhead is the distinct temperature gradient that sets up in the heat of the summer. By mid-August, there can be as much as a 15 °F temperature difference between the surface and bottom. This cool, deep-water pocket is what adult steelhead seek when taking a break from migrating up the Columbia River.

It's common for hardcore anglers to use a ferry system to protect preferred anchor spots when steelhead fishing gets hot. It works like this. One boat stays on anchor while relying on friends (or a small pram) to shuttle provisions and anglers back-and-forth to shore, or to use the public restroom. Which leads to the story of a boater's wife desiring something more refined than a small bucket to accommodate a call of nature. Her insensitive husband, fearing that he would lose his place, refused to pull up anchor. After bearing witness to several minutes of animated discussion, an adjacent boater cut loose, motored alongside and took her to shore. Needless to say, she did not return.

Leroy and I arrived on the scene at Drano Lake one afternoon and immediately anchored in a cluster of boats, choosing not to jockey for position in the dark. With six other boats, including a pair of monster jet boats tied together, we formed a tight circle. Adding to the mix at twilight was a guy who arrived in an 8-foot pram powered by a tiny electric troll motor. After dropping his anchor in our casting lane, he merely excused, "That was rude of me."

Nobody complained. You could sense he had done the drill before.

Meanwhile, I missed three bobber-downs and Leroy missed two within an hour of sunset. But the bite didn't begin in earnest until a waxing moon illuminated the placid surface like a Monet painting. The first signal of what was to come was a loud splash followed by the clank of net handle on the hull of a nearby alumi-num boat. Headlamps flashed on and off as surrounding boaters wrestled steelhead to submission. In between these brief fren-zied events, all was quiet. Sensing a bite-fest, I threaded on a fresh shrimp, set my bobber stop at 20 feet and casted upwind. Meanwhile, it had been a long day with no reward for Leroy. He put his rod down to crawl into his sleeping bag while I studied my lighted bobber as it drifted slowly towards the Columbia Riv-er, partially obscured by wave chop. Sometime around midnight, while Leroy slept, I was rewarded for my patience when the faint light of my bobber winked off like a burned-out Christmas tree bulb. A pull-down! Frantically reeling to recover slack line, I set the hook on a B-run steelhead. Perhaps confused in the dark, the compliant 12-pounder did not struggle until reaching the side of our boat. After kicking Leroy's sleeping bag to motivate his as-sistance, he managed to scoop up the fish wearing nothing but his best tidy whities.

My adrenaline was up leaving no choice but to return to casting. However, Leroy was not sufficiently impressed to join me. He crawled back in his bag. Still at it 2 hours later, I was rewarded with another bobber-down. Once again, Leroy got up without complaining to net my catch in his underwear. However, this time he dropped the big hatchery steelie and dripping wet net on my sleeping bag. "It's all yours," he said.

I marked my catch card and called it a night. As I recall, day-light came way too early.

CARTON OF WORMS

ON MY WAY TO the Walla Walla River to fish for steelhead, I stopped at the 76 Conoco-Phillips "Rocket Mart" to fill the gas tank and pick up a carton of worms. Normally I was down the road before sunup, but this frosty January trip lacked the same sense of urgency that motivated earlier in the season.

Three neon signs at the convenience store entrance beckoned to the masses: "ATM," "Lotto," "Sandwiches." Entering, I found the desk clerk with his back to the counter steaming a latte for a weight-challenged young woman clad in open-toed sandals, plaid flannel pajama pants and a faux leather jacket. I couldn't help but reflect on what some people wear in public.

Rather than interrupt the process, I headed for the back cooler, skirting hotdogs rotating in a glass panel oven, racks of chips, candy bars and Hostess desserts. After a quick survey of discount beer, I came up empty to walk back to the front. "Do you have worms?" I asked.

"If we do, they are at the bottom of shelf 10," the clerk replied.

I returned to the back cooler. At the bottom left hand corner of shelf 10 were several small white Styrofoam cups stacked three high. I would have recognized them as being worm cartons if I had bothered to bend over and look. The oversight reminded of previous searches of the home refrigerator where food items didn't hit me in the face at first pass. "Why don't you look a little harder?" my wife Nancy would admonish when I asked for help locating obvious refrigerator items.

Unfortunately, the worms were old. Their expiration date, if there had been one, was long past due. In fact, they were assimilated into the compost packing material. Cold air wafted out the deli case door as I desperately pawed through containers one-by-one, peeling off brittle plastic lids to examine a mixture of dirt, gray newsprint fiber and rotten worm slime. Nearing the end of the second stack of containers, a worm showed its foolish head above the packing material. I poked. It moved. My heart skipped a beat. A deeper probe revealed more live wrigglers. Mission accomplished! I had backup bait to complement my meager supply of roe.

Feeling culpable about the handful of loose worm bedding left scattered about the otherwise spotless linoleum floor, I moved quickly to the front of the store. If there's one thing my mother tried to reinforce during my formative years, it was to clean up after myself.

"Most of your worms are dead," I told the clean-faced young clerk, placing the container on the counter.

"Going walleye fishing?" he asked, ringing up the worms.

"Actually, steelhead," I replied. "Planned to take Thursday off but didn't because of rain and high winds."

"Where you heading?"

"Tucannon River."

It turned out he had fished at nearby Lyons Ferry the previous weekend. "I didn't catch anything," he shared. "Wish I had a boat to fish off the mouth of the Tuke. Clearwater should also be good."

"Or the Grand Ronde if you're willing to put in 4 hours on the road," I replied, thinking this guy knows his steelhead. I couldn't imagine anything worse than being stuck working in a mini-mart for minimum wage when you could be fishing.

Sensing I was ready to leave, the clerk ended with, "Well, they'll be in the river if they're anywhere. It's that time of year."

That's when my guilty conscience finally got the best of me. "Sorry about the mess I made in the back of the store," I said. "I had to sort through a bunch of cartons to find any live worms."

"That's okay. I'll clean it up later when I'm not making espressos. Good luck fishing."

If we could all be that benevolent.

Partners of the Zodiac

ᶫ

SOME FISHING BUDDIES are more of a challenge than they are worth. Indeed, the list of things that can bring conflict to a fishing trip is endless. For example, it's amazing how many times I've heard, "I didn't bring lunch." Translation: "Don't worry about poor old me sitting here without anything for the next 6 hours while you eat your sandwich." Then there's always, "Mind if I have one of your premium beers?" Does "I'm running light on gear" sound familiar?

While having such essentials as food, beverage and tackle contribute to the success of a trip; there are more serious matters to consider when evaluating the relative worth of a fishing buddy. For instance, do you notice his anxiety around simple tasks such as netting a fish? Maybe you milk a fight, but your buddy likes to horse his fish to the boat in no more time than it takes to reel up the downrigger? Don't forget the emotional cost of someone who hogs the tiller, trolling in the same mindless place, while you prefer to change locales at least once a week.

Have I got your attention yet? Believe me, despite popular opinion, opposites do not always attract. If any of these situations strike close to home, it's time to expand your awareness. I'm not advocating hairdresser cosmetology or incense burning, rather the basics of getting a derailed fishing relationship back on track. Alternatively, it might be time to jettison the bony-butt, nose-picker of a pseudo-buddy into the ozone and find someone that appreciates your angling talent for what you imagine it to be.

Let's start with the basics of a good relationship. For centuries, feelings between two people have been tracked through signs of the zodiac. Trust me on this one. Alignment of the sun, moon and stars has far more influence on your life than a random fruitcake at Christmas.

For example, I am a late September Libra. According to zodiac charts, my strongest virtues are diplomacy, tact, charm and social grace. My most negative trait is indecision. My deepest need is love and harmony. In other words, I get along with most anyone. A weakness is working at it too hard. Another way of saying it is I sometimes hate myself in the morning. More than once, I have screwed myself over by letting others have their way at my expense. Like giving a buddy first shot at a premium drift spot. What's that all about anyway? Let him figure it out on his own next time (reverting to the dark side of Libra).

Unfortunately, the stars suggest I need a partner in order to be at my best and to feel fulfilled. While I admit to enjoying the company of others, I also crave the freedom of fishing when and where I want without having to play off another person. Being a Libra can be complicated.

Signs of greatest compatibility within my zodiac are Gemini and Aquarius. Virgos are also considered harmonious while Pisces are off my list because they are "turbulent." Those of greatest incompatibility are Cancer and Capricorn, although the latter sign is considered most helpful for emotional support. Accordingly, a Capricorn should be left at home but sought out for consolation after a bad fishing day.

A recent situation with Leroy (a Sagittarius) shed some light on our relationship. It so happened he caught a small sockeye salmon, the tastiest of all Pacific salmon, after 18 hours of trolling. Immediately upon bonking it, he said, "It's not big enough to share."

Some would have thought his remark rude, but not me. I was eyeing his sockeye and he knew it. The timely comment cleared the air over whether to split the catch at the end of the trip. The fact we often argue like two old ladies fighting for bargains at a Wal-Mart holiday sale is beside the point. I took Leroy's choice of words to suggest that he gave deliberate thought about whether to offer me a filet. Only after pondering the size of the salmon, needs of his family and the fact I had three salmon of my own, did he reject the idea of sharing. It was just his way of saying, "Don't get any ideas!" Case closed due to Sagittarius clarity of thought. If not for his decisive action, this Libra might have pondered the possibilities for hours.

Freaked out with this glass bowl stuff? I don't blame you. However, for those doubting the occult, modern social science has developed more acceptable ways to profile human behavior. Most methods are designed to enable people to get along better in the work environment. A positive outcome of this approach is to categorize individuals into specific personality types based on input from themselves and others. I found out via one such a 360-degree assessment that I was an "amiable analytic." One explanation for the result is that I analyze people in order to get along with them. Whatever.

Outside of the corporate world, there are a plethora of web sites available to help one find a compatible companion. While some are thinly disguised as electronic pickup bars, others focus on relationships. One popular site goes so far as to assess "29 areas of compatibility" that supposedly lead to finding a perfect match. Survey questions relate to opinion on education, religion, feelings, values, life skills and communication style, among others. I recently logged on to get a feel of how things worked. Unfortunately, I had to choose the same-sex version of their on-line questionnaire so that my wife wouldn't think I planned to cheat on her. Despite logging out prior to completing the onerous form, I got tagged with a tricky set of e-mails that took several weeks to dissuade as assumptions about my sexual orientation went viral.

Finding a fishing buddy should not be so complicated as frequenting electronic chat rooms or placing ads in the back of the newspaper. Consequently, and for those of you without the patience to fill out a 295-question form, I developed a simple test of compatibility. My six questions, based on well-grounded principles of angling psychology, are designed to strengthen the amount of "unconditional positive regard" you have for your fishing buddy. (The phrase was stolen from a well-known psychologist to impress.) These questions get to the heart of the matter in no more time than it takes to boot up a 10-year-old PC.

If my approach sounds promising to your current situation, please continue. Building the foundation towards a long-term relationship may be easier than you think. Note that political and religious viewpoints are not included because fishing buddies don't converse about anything meaningful when on the water.

Question 1. Does your fishing buddy control the position and speed of the trolling motor to optimize presentation of your lure at the expense of his?

Question 2. Does he maintain a vigilant eye on your rod tip, equal to his, while you rustle a beer from the cooler?

Question 3. Does he routinely bring the net in position before you bring a fish to the boat?

Question 4. Does he readily share his party-sized bag of premium chips at lunchtime?

Question 5. Is he so hung up on fly-fishing that he cannot relate to casting roe (or vice-versa)?

Question 6. Does he smile when you make a sexual innuendo well before the first cup of coffee has been poured?

I realize that sharing feelings is not easy. Thus, consider each answer carefully and reflect on the end result—connecting with the fishing buddy of your life. Too late, time is up! (Just joking. Remember we Libras are known for our quick wit.)

Seriously, take all the time you need, but more than four negative responses to the six questions should tell you something. Like you are facing the hind end of the mule. Not to say that changing a partner in midstream is an easy decision, but life is too short to fish with someone who does not share your deepest sensibilities. Meanwhile, bring on the smiling Buddha, but please stay the heck out of my favorite fishing spot. Empathy has its limits.

Secret Holes

CONSIDER THE FOLLOWING discordant scene on the Columbia River at the height of Chinook salmon season. While drifting downstream near what is known as the "300 area," I approached two boats trolling in close proximity. As I got closer, one boat driver cut his engine to pull alongside the other. "What the hell are you doing in my spot?" he yelled. "I've been fishing this place for over 20 years. The last thing I want to see is you here. Look at it this way. How would you feel if you came home and found me in bed with your wife?"

The second boat driver fired up his main motor and drove off without saying a word. Apparently he picked the wrong time to fish his buddy's secret fishing hole.

It's not hard to find other challenges to the Tenth Commandment that involve encroachment. For instance, one of my best friends guards a certain walleye hole like it's the crown jewel. If friend or stranger motors by, Archie snubs them. Archie's obsession runs so deep that he once arranged for a neighbor to report on use of the area.

Wanting to fish there at least once before I died, I confronted Archie at work. "It's been 2 years since you took me to your walleye hole," I said. "Seems like the statute of limitations should be over. Shouldn't I be able to fish it sometime without fear of reprisal?"

Rather than answer, Archie chewed on his lower lip and turned his gaze to the wall. That's when I realized my head-on question had hit a nerve. That despite imagining best intention I had crossed the line. Upon further reflection, why would he embrace a sneak fish trip to a place he had worked so hard to find? The last thing I wanted to do was alienate a good friend over a dumb walleye hole, but unfortunately it was too late to withdraw the question.

After a polite pause, Archie struck back with something near and dear to my heart, "What if I fished your favorite steelhead hole on the Walla Walla River?"

Taken aback, I took a deep breath to collect my thoughts. "It's a free country," I replied. "I wouldn't be happy if I showed up first thing in the morning to find you with a fish on the bank, but I wouldn't excommunicate you over it either."

It was a safe answer. The truth was all my so-called secret steelhead holes are fairly dynamic. They come and go with each major high-water event. The only way anyone would find all of them would be to follow me around on a daily basis. I could provide you with GPS coordinates and a pre-season map but you would become disillusioned long before figuring out exactly where to fish on your own. Regardless, I got Archie's point. A true friend would never fish another person's secret fishing hole without permission. Or pick from their secret mushroom patch, for that matter.

There are other examples where I've been accused of leaking information about a revered location. The first time Leroy laid into me was when he spotted two of my buddies trolling off the mouth of the Yakima River a week after he shared catching two coho salmon there. "I can't believe you told your friends about my fish!" he said.

I argued that people had been fishing for salmon off the mouth of the Yakima River for years. It was not a secret hole. But Leroy didn't shut up until I produced a copy of a scientific paper published in 1895. In the paper, a local resident reported catching his first salmon of the season near the mouth of the Yakima River. (More than a century before Leroy "discovered it.") And unlike Leroy, the historical angler revealed his secret method, "The salmon bite readily at a spoon ... they are caught by trolling only."

Perhaps feeling remorse over the unfounded Yakima River accusation, or perhaps not, Leroy took me to another secret fishing place. This one was divulged during a trip to Rimrock Lake in pursuit of kokanee, a 115-mile drive that instead yielded a dozen bait-stealing suckers.

"My uncle used to take me there," Leroy said, offering up the secret fishing spot as partial mitigation for a kokanee trip gone bad. "He made me promise not to taken anyone else. I figure I can show you since he's been dead for 2 years now. But you've got to promise not to write about it."

Going along with the opportunity to learn something new, I promised not to write about this 2500-foot elevation, Naches River watershed pond, off U.S. Forest Service Road #1203 where cutthroat, rainbow and bull trout resided.

Once Leroy made his mind up to let me in on the family secret, he had no problem giving it up. "It's a short hike," he shared. "Not visible from the road."

Created the image of a pleasant hike on a shaded trail leading through tall tamarack and sunbeam-lit aspen.

"Did you bring your fly rod?" he added.

Created the image of monster trout dimpling the surface of a willow-lined beaver pond fed by a gin-clear mountain spring.

But what I found after testing my rear shocks several miles up a rutted dirt road was much different. This secret hole was not in the same category as previously disclosed sanctuaries. Aesthetically, the site was a disaster. We parked at the edge of an open area pock-marked with cow pies and bull thistle. The centerpiece was a large fire pit built from discarded concrete blocks and lined with crushed beer cans. A badly eroded trail, twisting through wild rose and stunted ponderosa pine, led to a turbid, silt-bottom pond devoid of fish as near as I could tell after standing in the hot sun to watch my bobber float aimlessly for three long hours.

I'm not one to kiss and tell, but the status of that secret hole, I sensed, was elevated in his mind by a huge dose of nostalgia. All I could think of was that Leroy had been treated to all the Cheetos, M&Ms and Nehi orange soda he wanted when accompanying his uncle on fishing trips to this barren beaver pond. I couldn't argue whether the secret hole meant something 30 years ago, but visiting it was no longer worth the price of gas.

These are but a few examples of events leading to controversy after I apparently breached the trust of a fishing buddy. Unfortunately, my wife has had to endure a lifetime of listening to me attempt to ease my conscience. But not until after the last incident with Leroy did she offer closure on the topic. "Give me a break," she said. "Your friends have no grounds for complaining. First of all, who's to say they're the only ones who know about the spot? Second, if they tell someone about their secret, then they are giving it up. By all rights, it's now your place or anyone else's place to try."

Having been an elementary school teacher for 19 years, she is well qualified to provide pragmatic solutions for childish disputes. Her rationale suits me fine. The truth is, most anglers lack the willpower to keep a secret. For that reason, you shouldn't put a fishing buddy in the position of knowing your secret fishing hole unless you are prepared to "give it up."

SWIMMING WITH DOLPHINS

DROPPING THE TAILGATE of my truck down with a loud clang, I pulled on neoprene waders stiff from being hung in the garage all summer. A warm October wind blew hard across the desert landscape obscuring Rattlesnake Mountain with a thick cloud of dust. I stood on the bank above the Yakima River looking for a path to the shoreline. Blocking my way was a concrete-lined irrigation canal filled with slow-moving water. I slid down the slope and eased in up to my armpits. It took all of my concentration to tiptoe safely across the canal and crawl out the other side. My vest stayed dry, no gear floated free and my waders didn't leak. Everything added up to good luck.

The well-trodden path to the river was full of an assortment of pitfalls that included rusty fence wire, old tires and muskrat holes. Empty beer cans and Styrofoam bait containers added to the clutter. Archie was backing up to shore, his rod bowed to the firm pull of a thrashing salmon. Hurrying to get into the action, I tripped and nosedived into a small clump of cattail. Archie didn't notice. But then, he had seen it all before.

We were in the middle of southeastern Washington sagebrush country on the lower Yakima River. Our target was fall Chinook salmon that return every year in early September. A mile upstream, water spilled over Horn Rapids Dam, a place known as "Wanawish" by the local Wanapum Indian tribe. The old and the new mix here where tribal fishers and wooden fishing platforms coexist with sport anglers.

I knelt down to select a 3/0 hook adorned with orange yarn from my belly pack. In my haste to get started, I popped the tip guide off my spinning rod only to have it disappear like a bad dream in a loose matting of reed canary grass and horsetail. Luckily, Archie, with the eyesight of a 30-something, found the errant piece of chrome. I twisted the guide on and was back in business.

By the time I rigged up, Archie was back at work, crotch deep in the river and casting low into the wind. Following his lead, I worked my way across algae-crusted rocks as slick as snot. The wind had increased in ferocity whipping the water's surface into a white-capped froth and sending sheets of spray against my chest. When I stopped to brace myself in the strong current, Archie pointed and yelled, "That's the honey hole!"

I took his word for it having no clue how to read the water under such breezy conditions. When I quartered a long cast upstream, the strong southwest wind caught my slack and looped line over Archie's head and shoulders. "I'll get better," I yelled.

Archie shrugged indifferently, concentrating on his drift. He rarely got ruffled when fish were biting, especially when working a wad of chew. I made a short low cast into the wind and let my ball of roe sink in the shallow riffle. After two quick taps, I got the hint and jerked hard, but came up empty. It was too little, too late.

Putting on a fresh gob of golf-ball sized roe, I cast twice more to the same spot before getting a no-nonsense strike that every fisherman appreciates. The no-brainer take started with a solid chomp followed by tight line moving crosscurrent in a hurry. When I set the hook, the battle was on. It felt heavy, but I had not hooked anything of size in over two months, so what did I know? The salmon peeled off half the line on my spool before taking a right turn to churn up the shallows on the far bank. Almost like it got carried away with its escape plan. Following the fish downstream, I slipped on a rock and fell on my side. Despite a fresh gallon of water in my waders and a badly bruised knee, I managed to pump the deep-bodied salmon into the shallows. My battered pride was redeemed after I landed the 25-pound, scarlet-sided specimen with a glorious kype. Extracting the hook from the corner of its toothy mouth, I yelled, "Spawn until you die!"

Archie and I hooked several more Chinook salmon in the next 3 hours. In between "takes" and "gnashes," salmon rolled and splashed around us. They slashed and cavorted on the surface as if mirroring underwater combat drills. One leapt through rolling waves like a wind surfer trying for big air. Some fish bore deep and ran long after they were hooked. Others bulldogged close and shook their heads until subdued.

I hooked a small salmon that jumped eight times before I finally landed it. The cause of its fighting prowess was a hook stuck in the orbit of its eye. Towards the end of the day, I caught two small bucks identical in every feature including a two-tone silver-gray side, caudal peduncle splashed with red and a slight bend of the snout. I couldn't help but wonder if they were siblings returning to their natal place to spawn.

Most salmon were less than a month from spawning. I reeled in one brown and red specimen and yelled, "Chrome-bright."

Archie replied, "Sea lice still hanging off the vent."

The not-so-prime condition of these salmon didn't matter. We suffered no gastrointestinal panic, no leg quiver or no desire to light up a smoke to calm nerves when a fish got off. It was all about the thrill of the strike. We each kept one salmon, most likely the last of the year. Their orange flesh had deteriorated to a blonde tone, but it was still full of fat. They would smoke up fine after an overnight soak in brown sugar and salt.

I couldn't help wonder what made these late run salmon attack bait with such reckless abandonment. Was it displacement behavior, i.e., the result of excess nervous energy available after requirements for migration had been met? Surely, the instinct to defend their territory was part of it, but the readiness at which they attacked golf-ball sized clusters of roe made you wonder about strength of remnant feeding instinct.

There has continued to be highlights. Like the 39-pound salmon I caught on my birthday while fishing with my son-in-law Will. The big salmon plowed back-and-forth in a deep pool for over a half hour before I got a look at it. I almost had a heart attack when it jumped so close to douse me. Will's only comment, "You lucky bastard," stemmed not from malice but rather from having to bear witness to my charmed luck.

Leroy recently related another gem of a story. "Well, I was drifting eggs for salmon on the Yak, just downstream of where you like to stand. Two women were casting along the shore by the tree where you wade out. I started talking to them. One was from around here and the other said she worked at a large public aquarium on the East Coast. Anyway, I hooked this big Chinook and was fighting him when they waded down to watch. I didn't want to keep it so I asked them if they wanted it. One of them said, 'Sure, but wait while we go get a harness.'"

"Was that for you or the fish?" I asked.

Leroy laughed. "For the fish. Anyway, while one of them went to get it, the other one waded out to get behind the salmon but she fell in a hole and filled her waders. She crawled back to the bank and dumped most of the water out while I tired the salmon out. They told me to bring the fish to the bank and into the grass where it's dark. 'To quiet it down.'"

"It sounds like the woman from the East Coast had worked with dolphins or something," I said.

"Maybe," Leroy replied. "Anyway, I led the salmon to shore and they worked a small dog harness around it and hauled it out of the water. It was a big buck, over 30 pounds. You know how steep that dirt bank is leading up to the canal? They had no problem dragging my salmon right up the hill and to their rig."

It's hard to top that one although every year brings on more local color: bare-chested guys wading in Levis, stringers of dark salmon lying in the trail "curing" in the afternoon sun, 8-foot Jon boats that exceed load limits by at least 200 pounds. On other days, the number of empty Keystone Lights lining the bank and the tattoo-to-tooth ratio exceeds the national average. Despite these proletarian scenarios, fishing the Yak in early fall is a venue worth testing if for no other reason than to plant your feet firmly when desert winds blow hard.

POINTY HEAD

My FAVORITE THREE-SEASON fishing hat is a sweat-stained Titleist cap that was once white. (Ever heard of a lucky hat?) Similar to my skeletal form, it has shrunk with age. Consequently, the cap rests on top of my head, off-kilter, scrunched up like an old paper bag. I keep an eye out for suitable replacements but have had difficulty finding one that fits. A recent incident provides insight.

"That hat looks good on you." Jerry said.

We were standing around in Dave's unheated garage, trying to stay warm between hands of a game of Texas Hold'em. It was not my choice to take a break, but I lost all my chips on a particularly clever "all in" move by someone having better cards. Meanwhile, I picked up a worn brown wool cap lying on top of a pile of coats rather than steal another microbrew. The cap felt comfortable, but the garage lacked a mirror to see how it set on my head. "I think it's Brian's hat," I replied to Jerry. "I was curious to see if it fit. It's not easy to find the right hat when you've got a pointy head."

"I'm surprised that you knew you had a pointy head," Jerry said.

"I'd have to be pretty dense to not know something like that. It's like being born with a big nose or having ears that stick out. These things you figure out after awhile. All it takes is looking in the mirror and comparing yourself with others. In my case, a hat might look good when I first buy it, but sooner or later, it creeps up to perch on top of my pointy head like an over-stuffed cabbage."

As a former All-Star Little League baseball player, I imagined looking sharp in uniform, ball cap included. I can attest to shaping the bill and crown of a baseball hat to look cool. However upon review of old family photos, this state-of-affairs does not appear to be the case. The black-and-white images captured either a hat cocked back or one perched crooked on my head. Perhaps it was my butt that attracted young female fans?

I placed Brian's cap back on the pile of coats and pondered my pointy head. Skull shape is never an issue on the stream because when it comes to fishing, hat style comes down to the basics. You need cover gear to shade your eyes from the sun, shield your head from rain, prevent ticks from burrowing into your scalp and protect from birds defecating on your head. Color is important only if there is a requirement for a fishing buddy to identify you from a distance. Having a logo that relates to the sport of angling is a bonus.

My older brother Dusty favors a red paisley scarf wrapped around his forehead when he's fishing. He used to wear a retro-green Oregon Trout ball cap, but it blew off his head during a raft trip on the Deschutes River and was lost. In hindsight, the cap either wasn't cinched down tight or pointy heads run in the family.

For now, I'm sticking with my old ball cap. I've never been a fan of safari-style headgear and straw cowboy hats are too much of a challenge when the wind blows. The truth is, not worrying about style points makes fishing simpler. Reflection off the water is all the flattery I need.

DID YOU READ THE REGS?

I ADMIT TO HAVING EARNED a speeding ticket or two, but never imagined I would find myself on the wrong end of a fish and game law after five decades of pursuing the noble mountain whitefish.

It had been over a month since Leroy and I fished together which meant time was ripe for another get together. Our last trip was a bust due to high winds that blew us off the Columbia River before we hooked a single fish. The only positive part about the experience was I got to sleep in and Leroy took his boat. Not that I was especially lonely for his company, but we needed something good to happen between us. Either that, or reevaluate the relationship.

Planning the next fishing trip was a typical DDD-Leroy affair, starting with my leading question, "Want to go fishing?" and his predictable response, "Maybe. What were you thinking?"

This brief exchange ensued a series of e-mails that went back-and-forth like two ballroom dancers who knew all the moves but didn't want to yield to the other's lead. I postured for a walleye trip having given up on steelhead for the year. Leroy favored whitefish hoping to fill his smoker. We gained little ground on the objective before I finally relented to call him at work.

"Made up your mind yet?" I asked.

"What are you thinking?" he replied.

"I'd like to try walleye fishing but I don't want to go to Wallula. It gets too much wind this time of year. I'm thinking someplace different, like White Bluffs, would be interesting. I'll take my boat."

"Nothing personal," he said, "You know how to catch walleye okay. But I think I've learned all I can from you on the topic."

"What you're saying is the quality of dog food slopping out of my bowl is not worth your time to eat?"

"Something like that," he replied. "I don't want to devote an entire day to walleye fishing. Besides, I thought you were going to scope out the lower Yak for whitefish."

"I was but I decided to do yard work instead. I don't need to practice fishing for whities just so you feel comfortable with the concept. Plus I electroshocked the stretch downstream of Horn Rapids Dam once so know where whitefish hold out for the winter."

"Whitefish still has my vote," Leroy reinforced. "I'll meet you at your place since it's on the way."

With what and where to fish for solved, the only thing left was figuring out when. The challenge, as always, was I liked to sleep in while Leroy was a habitual 4 a.m. riser. Rather than revisit the same old argument, I hatched an idea. "It's still freezing overnight," I declared. "I can't see starting before 9. Tell you what, show up at 8:30 and I'll fix you pancakes."

"Sounds great. See you then," he said, hanging up after the shortest negotiation of start time in the history of DDD and Leroy.

Saturday morning came with clear skies and a hard frost. I had a pot of strong coffee perking and the griddle was hot when Leroy's truck rolled to a stop in front of the house. "The Yak came up 1000 cfs since yesterday," I reported, greeting him at the front door. "Finding a place on the bank to stand could be a challenge."

"All I need is two or three fish to fill my smoker," Leroy replied. "I'm counting on you to help get them."

Satiated after wolfing down a plateful of buttermilk pancakes with a sausage patty on the side, we loaded our gear and headed for the river. It was an easy 10-minute drive to the unimproved launch off Snively Road where we scoped access to the river. "The shallow tailout above that island is a good holding area for whitefish," I said pointing towards a river swollen and off-color from snowmelt. "There's a trail through the blackberries and poison oak here someplace that leads down to the river."

Leroy and I were bundled up in hooded sweatshirts and stocking caps to combat a morning chill that clung to frosted ground. I recalled fishing the Yakima in October for Chinook salmon when the shoreline was vibrant with gold, orange and red hues of autumn. On this day, the landscape was bleak and dull. Trees were bare and reed canary grass crumpled and rotting, yet it felt good to be out of the house with fishing rod in hand.

While we gazed at the surround waiting for inspiration, a white Ford pickup truck turned off the gravel access road and pulled alongside. The logo on the driver's side door read "WDFW." The badge on the chest of the uniformed man behind the wheel said "Wildlife Enforcement Officer."

"What's up guys?" he asked through the rolled-down window.

"Not much," I replied, for the first time acutely aware of the "No Trespassing" sign I was straddling. "We're looking for a path to the river to try for whitefish."

"Do you know the river is closed to fishing?"

"What? Since when?" I asked.

"Since the first of November," the officer replied, removing his dark glasses to scrutinize us.

"Really. Even for whitefish?"

"Yup. The only part open is upstream of the Highway 223 Bridge."

"Where's that?"

"Up by Sunnyside-Granger."

"That's way upstream," I said. "We used to be able to fish for whitefish here in January. When did the rules change?"

"About 5 years ago."

"Oh."

Perhaps to confirm we weren't whitefish poachers, Leroy offered, "I know about the size 14 hook rule. I fished the upper Yakima last week. It was open."

"Well it's not open down here," the officer retorted, his once friendly tone hinting exasperation at our ignorance. "I'll let you off this time, but maybe you should read the regulations before you plan your next fishing trip."

With that, he rolled up his window and drove off leaving Leroy and I to ponder the situation. "Looks like I've got time to butcher a chicken or two before it gets dark," Leroy said. "It's a good thing I got pancakes out of the deal."

Needless to say, the topic of fishing together has not come up recently.

MAKING FISH SAUSAGE

NOT UNTIL MY VEGETARIAN brother-in-law showed up at Thanksgiving dinner with a holiday plate full of salmon sausage did I think about doing some of the same. Frankly speaking, I didn't like the way he rolled the mixture in little dooly balls, then wrapped them with foil before parboiling the weird-shaped fish wiener like some kind of poached egg delight. I wanted to create a manlier version. Something stuffed in casing to be grilled over hot coals with habanera compote on the side and washed down with Guinness stout.

I should mention that I am a lover of domestic sausage having eaten everything from Wisconsin's finest to Jimmy Dean's grocery store patties, which aren't bad by the way. But what I savor most is sausage made from wild game such as venison or duck to the point I have been known to beg for the 2-year-old freezer-burned variety from friends that kill Bambi and Daffy at great frequency.

Despite having an abundance of German heritage hiding somewhere in the woodpile, there was no tradition of sausage making in my family. All animal protein came straight from the grocery store. Consequently, making fish sausage was plowing new ground. I started my quest with a quick Internet search. What was revealed were fish recipes dating back to 1738. Reviews of upscale dining establishments further validated the role of fish sausage as fine cuisine.

Armed with this newfound knowledge, the next step was to find a supply of casing. Casing is a flattering word for animal gut. It's the smooth elastic tissue that lower digestive tracts are made of. Think colonoscopy.

Figuring on making a party-sized pile of salmon hotdogs, I located a butcher shop that sold animal casing. A 1-pound bag – the only size available – cost $30. Unfortunately, it came frozen solid and wrapped in thick white paper, providing no clue what it looked like. "How many feet are there in the package?" I asked the butcher.

"Enough to make 125 pounds of sausage," he replied.

Given I had 15 pounds of salmon filets languishing in the deep freeze, casing was no longer critical path. The only other advice offered before I walked out the door was from the shop girl who pointed to a stack of plump frankfurters languishing in the meat case. "We use the same casing to make those."

I was so excited that I opened up the little bundle of frozen gut as soon as I got home. It reminded me of spider webbing. Frankfurters, heck! How could you possibly stuff ground fish meat into such tiny little strands of silly putty? I could barely stretch it over the end of a No. 2 pencil. Finding an opening was more of a challenge than high school sex. This particular exercise in futility was setting up to be a hand job with sausage patties not a preferred option.

Temporarily setting aside the challenge of exactly how to stuff the meat into the still-frozen casing, I poached the Chinook salmon in a large stainless steel pot until the meat flaked, removed the skin and mashed the product with a fork until it achieved the consistency of a tuna fish sandwich. So far, I was in complete control having operated in a similar mode prior.

I let the meat cool, added spices and other key ingredients before using a wooden spoon to mix in a bowl. A food processor would have been a better option, but I tend to be old school. Throughout the entire process, I was careful to keep the splatter of fish to a minimum while the family dog posed vigilantly between my legs, knowing that raw salmon can carry *Salmonella*, a disease deadly to canines.

Turning the blended fish mixture into a sausage link was the next step. However, it soon became evident that spreading tiny gut tissue apart by hand was not a job for someone with poor eyesight and fat fingers. As further evidence of my resourcefulness, I solved the problem by shoving bits of salmon mixture into the miniscule opening with well-coordinated movement of my thumb and forefinger. Working patiently in this manner, it took an hour to construct one 3-inch long sausage.

One thought was that size does matter when it comes to sausage. Another thought was that at the current rate, the first batch of fish would not be packed into a string of links until midnight on day two. So I quit and watched football until my wife got home. She, being an excellent cook, might have a better idea.

"What did the instructions say?" Nancy asked.

The implication hurt but I came back with a strong answer. "There are no directions. The only thing provided is a list of ingredients and that you should stuff the fish into hog or sheep casing."

"Did you ever think of looking in a cookbook?"

"What would they know about stuffing sausage?"

As it turned out, Jacques Pepin and his classic culinary guide *La Technique* saved me. Chef Jacque devoted six pages of text to making sausage. More important was a sequence of photos showing how to fill casing by hand. Most insightful was a photo demonstrating how to fit the casing to a water spigot in order to rinse and expand it. The method reminded of filling water balloons. The result reminded of a prophylactic. The end product, however, was a flexible expanded membrane far easier to handle than the spider web I started with. My quest for fish sausage took on renewed faith.

All that remained was delivering the mashed up product into a somewhat expanded casing. This part of the process took some ingenuity. First, I filled a plastic funnel used to change oil on my vintage sports car with salmon meat. Then I stretched the end of the casing over the tip of the funnel. Finally, using a wooden dowel as a piston, I forced the salmon mixture from the funnel into the casing. Once I got the hang of it, I manufactured a modest string of man-sized links resembling anemic bratwurst

Don't expect the skin-popping bite of a frankfurter when you chomp a fish dog. The only thing a butcher-shop "all meat" frank has in common with a fish hotdog is the casing. After a 200-mile swim up the Columbia River, salmon have less than half the fat content of Italian sausage. Despite leaving no juice on the lip, the final product has proven to be a worthy companion to smoked steelhead, elk jerky and duck pepperoni at the holiday snack table. It's something that can be enjoyed by carnivores and vegetarians alike.

THERE IS A FISH GOD

U

I ADMIT TO PRAYING for things that others might consider frivolous, a behavior traceable to a warm fall day early in my angling career when I couldn't buy a bite and returning to camp without a fish was not an option. Wading across a shallow riffle, I closed my eyes and reached out for assistance, using a well-honed phrase reserved for desperate moments, "Please God let me catch a fish."

Lo and behold, a small rainbow trout shot out from behind a rock to strike the #12 gray hackle left skidding on the water's surface. One might argue the fish was fascinated by action of the fly; however, I can think of no other plausible explanation than divine intervention.

I will attest to religion doing an admirable job of filling in questions science leaves unanswered based on several years of bible study during my formative years. A fair amount of faith-based stuff sinks in no matter how much daydream power a person might employ to get past the Dead Sea and topics of equal viability. So what if some believers only go to the well in time of great need, such as when fish aren't biting?

I'm not knocking religion. Religion is useful if for no other reason than it provides answers for events for which there is no logical explanation. Making sense of a bad situation allows people to move along in their life. I also support most religious notions, in particular ones about being nice to our fellow men. The world needs more nice people.

But this story is about fishing. In sharp contrast to those residing deep within the fold of organized religion, my friend Leroy is so ingrained in the scientific method that he believes the only thing between him and catching more fish is having more data. This mindset comes by way of his status as a bigwig scientist at a large think tank. While there is no denying that more information makes for a better angler, not all piscatorial outcomes are readily explained by science. At least that's what I tell him after I guide him to a secret hotspot and we return home skunked.

Leroy and I have had our share of good days and bad days. Most bad days involved searching for large salmon to put in the box. On one such bad day, we trolled shallow when we observed salmon surfacing and we trolled deep where targets were seen on the fish finder. We used cut-plug herring with a variety of high-tech flashers to entice and stimulate. We rubbed Smelly Jelly on Magnum Wiggle Warts and wrapped Kwikfish with fresh sardine to impart scent. We trolled fast, we trolled slow. We paid acute attention to our rods and we ignored them. We ate snacks and we peed off the bow of the boat. None of these proven fish-catching techniques worked.

Around 8 p.m., on this hot August evening, the sun slipped behind the granite-lined hills above the quiet town of Brewster, Washington. It was now or never. We had entered the "magic hour." This special time occurs at the end of each day when wind lessens, light fades and fish become more active as if to expend a final burst of energy before they settle down for the night. Whether from pure despair or the need to generate hope, Leroy did something that I had never seen him do before: he offered up a prayer to the mighty fish gods.

This pious turn of events caught me by surprise. You see, Leroy had not mentioned religious preference in more than a decade of our fishing together. The topic hadn't come up despite countless hours spent driving back-and-forth to remote locations when sheer boredom might have led to either of us to slip up and bare our soul. But if Leroy had asked, I would have admitted to being raised a rogue Methodist. I might have even mentioned reading the entire bible (Abridged Version) from cover to cover as a Boy Scout in order to earn the coveted God and Country award. But he never asked. And as for Leroy, his religious preference has always been fishing. His idea of a perfect Sunday morning service has always been to give thanks at the "Church of the Stream."

So I was faced with a dilemma. If previous religious upbringing had taught me anything, it taught me to reserve prayer only for moments of true suffering. This particular situation did not appear to qualify. Plus, we had another day to fish and I still had a few more fish-catching tricks up my sleeve. And finally, if I were to pray, it would be done silently and not in a group setting.

Nonetheless, Leroy's dominant personality persevered. I mumbled along like the sheep I was as he raised a warm can of Pabst Blue Ribbon to the setting sun and chanted, "Oh, great God of Chinooks, please grant us a fish for we have been arrogant."

I must admit that Leroy's choice of words reminded me of all the great closing prayers I had heard in my youth. Closing was always my favorite part of the service because it was the time I was set free of the ties that bound me to the pew to join up with heathen friends who spent Sunday mornings playing baseball and kick the can. Suddenly, my senses felt alive. Red and gold rays of sunlight burst through the smoky haze like bottle-rockets on the Fourth of July. The bait cooler emanated with odors of a noon-time Manhattan delicatessen and passing semi-trucks resonated tunes reminding of YoYo Ma at the cello.

These supreme events were merely an omen that the best was yet to come for no sooner did we sit down and resume blank stares across the wide expanse of Lake Rufus Woods when Leroy's rod tip went down. Fish on! He jumped up, set the hook and horsed the salmon to the net like there was no tomorrow.

At the risk of coming off like a circus-tent preacher, the only plausible explanation for a salmon to take final communion on Leroy's lure was that a higher being had responded to his desperate plea for help. Divine intervention. The outcome also reinforced that if neither science nor luck can provide the upper hand on small-brained salmon, a person might consider unleashing the power of prayer.

Driving out of town the next morning, I reminded Leroy of an earlier conversation. "You said you didn't care if I caught all the fish on this trip as long as we came home with something in the ice box. I didn't believe you. There was no way that I could be generous enough to feel good about you catching all the fish. Now it appears a higher being rewarded you for having a benevolent attitude, while punishing me for selfish thought."

"I would tend to agree with you," he replied. "However, please don't tell my wife I was invoking religious thoughts. She might try to get me to go to church."

I promised to keep his wife out of it if he gave me a fish to take home. Leroy readily complied. After all, the small concession more than made up for the lesson in faith.

FISH MANURE

WANDERING INTO A LOCAL plant nursery in early March, I looked to jumpstart my spring vegetable garden with a fresh complement of organic fertilizer. The outside entrance tempted with signs of spring: multicolored pansies, paper bags filled seed potatoes, bundles of onions, potted perennials, flowering fruit trees. Just inside the front door, lined up on the wall opposite the front counter, were bags of steer manure, chicken manure and compost. After carefully analyzing the benefits of each, I settled on chicken manure (the most expensive). The swing vote for my choice was pleasant memories raising a small flock of banties in our family's urban backyard. "I like the fact it's concentrated," I told the clerk. "If I need more fertilizer, there is always horse manure down the road to be had for 15 minutes of shoveling."

Leaning on the counter was a well-dressed older gentleman with an impressive handlebar mustache, tips neatly waxed to extend just short of his ear lobes. Having overhead the conversation, he asked, "Why not catfish manure?" Before quickly adding, "That's my nickname."

"You mean manure?" I replied, with a straight face.

He laughed. "No! It's catfish. But some folks say I'm full of manure."

"You set yourself up for that one," I said. "It was a softball toss."

While the clerk rang up my purchase, I went on to share a story with the mustached stranger. "Several years back I had a job sampling fish in the Hanford Reach. One spring day we caught nearly 50 suckers in a gill net, so I brought them home to bury in shallow trenches similar to how Indians taught the Pilgrims. The only problem was the neighbor's dog digging up the rotting carcasses to roll in. Once I figured out how to keep the dog out of my garden, it was some of the tallest corn ever."

Not to be outdone, the stranger leaned against the counter to reciprocate with a tale of a big channel cat he pulled from a deep hole in the lower Yakima River. "That one went into the oven though, not the garden," he concluded.

While driving off, I couldn't help wonder if his fishy nickname was due to the fancy mustache or his angling prowess for whisker cats.

ON RETIREMENT

YESTERDAY WAS A PARTICULARLY good day for this recent retiree. On my morning walk to the mail box, I found a barely used tube of Chap Stick, struck up a conversation with a man walking a yellow cat on a leash and admired a neighbor putting up new siding.

Being retired is not always this exciting. Some days I go fishing. Sadly, however, the first day of retirement was indicative of what was to come. As I recall, it was mid-week, the second of June. Channel cats were spawning so I took a retired friend to fish cut bait under slip bobber in the Palouse River. I towed my boat to the Lyons Ferry Marina, crossed the Snake River, plowed through a half-mile-long mud flat with my motor on half tilt and threaded up the narrow river channel to find a small fleet of boats with two or three old guys in each. Motoring up to a camo-colored Jon boat, I announced, "It's my first day of retirement. What's with all the people?"

A fat bald-headed man sitting under a large red umbrella with loose spokes replied, "Welcome to our world."

That day and several more like it leave little doubt that retirement ain't always fishing without competition. There are a lot of retired people out there with fishing on their minds. Add in the 10% or so unemployed or furloughed and workers having flexible schedules, and angler traffic on some waterways is considerable during the average work week.

There were other things I had not factored in to retirement planning. Probably the least underestimated part of my retirement budget was gas. It's a rare trip that does not require putting gas in my truck. Then, imagine how quickly road miles add up when you fish three or four times a week instead of once or twice on the weekend. Not to mention more boat time. I know. You weep for me.

"Do you have any idea what you spent on gas last month?" Nancy said, while sorting out our monthly bills.

"$300?" I replied.

"More like $800."

"I guess I hit the river pretty hard for salmon. My truck mileage ain't so good either when I pull the boat and trailer. And I did top up the boat more than once."

To reconstruct, the tally for that October included three trips to the cabin to fly fish for rainbow trout, two trips to the Hanford Reach to troll for fall Chinook salmon and one trip to McNary Dam for summer steelhead. This schedule paled in comparison to the previous December when I clocked more than 5,000 miles chasing steelhead from one end of the state to another. So much for my new truck being a secondary vehicle.

I often think about having a fishing car, something getting good gas mileage yet with room for all my gear. Leroy plans to fix up his wife's Honda Odyssey for a fishing car when he retires. "It gets 26 mile per gallon," he said. "My truck gets 11 miles per gallon. It's a no-brainer."

I was quick to reply, "Good idea. You could take out the passenger seats and sleep in it. A 21st century hippy van."

Leroy recently shared about fishing for steelhead at Little Goose Dam, one of his favorite haunts. "Went fishing with the

Starbuck boys last weekend," he said. "It was red hot. Ten guys and seven fish. I was out of there by 9:30 a.m. with three fish."

"Sounds red hot for you, but not for at least five other guys if I do the math."

"Actually, six guys went home unhappy since another guy caught two."

I bring this story up because that's the day Leroy hit a deer as he raced down the narrow winding grade leading to the Snake River. The impact was hard enough to smash a headlamp and crack the front bumper of his wife's van. When he showed off the repair job, I couldn't help notice how he had artfully feathered in gray duct tape over the brown plastic bumper. I still maintain he mashed his future fishing van to improve chances for acceptance by long-standing members of the bobber-down crowd.

A close third on a long list of unanticipated retirement challenges was experiencing the wrath of my wife for frequent donut stops at a certain bakery. Just the other day, she remarked, "I found another white paper sack on the floorboard in the back of your truck. It appears that you use fishing as an excuse to buy donuts."

Although the salvo struck close to home, I managed to shrug it off. Unfortunately, she was not deterred, following up with, "Admit it. You are attracted to her."

I tried misdirection, seeing as how denial rarely works. Once again she read me like a cheap romance novel, something that happens every time I feign lack of interest in another woman. "You've gone in there with me enough times to know that's not true," I pleaded.

"If it wasn't true you could always go to another bakery where women are old and grouchy," she replied, with the assurance of a prosecuting attorney.

Knowing my goose was cooked I couldn't help but add, "I can't help the fact she makes the best apple fritters in town."

Indeed, her pastries have the perfect ratio of sugar to grease, resulting in a delicate flavor that is both crispy and sweet. They are intoxicating when hot off the oil and darn good when day-old cold, not that I can recall many lasting overnight.

Speaking of my favorite bakeshop, I recently stopped by to ease a guilty conscience. "I have a confession to make," I said to the alluring baker after waiting patiently for her to dole out a glazed treat to another attentive male customer.

"What do you mean?" she said, hands resting on hips.

"I bought a frosted cake donut from the Spudnut Shop last week."

"In that case, no free donut holes today," she said, charging me double for an apple fritter.

Okay. I admit to being in and out of trouble all my life. But, I usually shake it off and go on. So what if I appreciate a friendly smile with my coffee and donut? Not to mention that once a sweet-tooth retiree learns the difference between a hot glazed pastry from a neighborhood bakeshop and a sugar-deficient dough ball from a convenience store, he is hooked for life. I am well qualified to judge such matters having started off most fishing trips with a sack of donuts.

Such culinary addiction adds up three ways. First is the extra cost of a premium pastry. Second, is the expectation of fishing buddies to provide such on regular basis. And third, eating donuts leads to extra calories keeping you at your winter weight all year long

It's a vicious cycle. Fill the gas tank. Fish. Eat donuts. Fish some more. I can't seem to get off the merry go round. Still, I wouldn't trade a minute of retirement for even the best day at work.

REASONS TO FISH ALONE

I AM NOT A RECLUSE. You might even find me sociable based on the fact I have a large circle of friends. However, I sometimes chose to fish alone. It's not because I am self-centered (although I may be). The main reason has to do with divergent values. Like not putting up with a buddy who insists on bringing his dog along. You know how dogs end up after a day on the water? They are either wet, muddy or they stink from having rolled in a dead animal. And the worse they smell, the more they want to be in your lap.

Another category of debatable fishing companions is the cheapskate. I'm not a guide, but if I were, my fishing buddies would be paying at least $150 a day for services rendered. So why do some of them show up with no beer, no snacks and complain when I don't lead them to fish?

There are other behaviors that factor into the desire to fish alone. For example, I like to be on the move. That means no sitting on a log and no plunking from a lawn chair. This behavior pattern corresponds to what clinical psychologists characterize as "attention-deficit hyperactivity disorder." I remain in denial, with a caveat being lack of a professional diagnosis due to the era I grew up in.

Competing biorhythms can also complicate a shared fishing experience. Consider that I am not a morning person. I rise early only when necessary, for instance to beat a former fishing buddy to a secret hole. This relaxed attitude restricts the number of trips I take with early birds, insomniacs, morning people and others who get up without qualm to wait until first light. Forgive me, but their approach to fishing is too much like duck hunting.

It's also easier to rationalize getting skunked when fishing alone. I can take a mental break to hunt agates, admire native flora and fauna, or nap on the stream bank—all useful endeavors when fishing is slow. I can't do any of those things and maintain my self-respect when a fishing buddy is around.

Then there is the drive to-and-from a fishing location. It's important to me to play Jimi Hendrix if I feel like screaming guitar licks, Emmy Lou Harris if I need female attention, Merle Haggard if I want to feel like a good ol' boy or Brahams if I want to soar above it all. Which reminds one of my brother Daran's friendship tests was to tear off a chunk of dinner bread before passing the loaf to a casual date. If her reaction was to ask for a knife to cut the bread cleanly, he knew the relationship wouldn't last. The point being one of my friendship tests is your taste in music.

As a last resort to expand my list of faithful fishing buddies, I turned to family members. Unfortunately, I have used up most of my chits with siblings. They are burned out and refuse to come out to play. At family gatherings, they look the other way and start up conversation with someone else. You know you're being ignored when your sibling opens up the Good Book and they are not religious.

All through courtship and early matrimony, my wife was a faithful companion. She would get up at dawn and hike like a trooper through brush. She would ignore "No Trespassing" signs and out-maneuver pasture bulls to fish with me. Now she'll only go fishing if I promise she'll catch something and there is a public restroom within 50 yards.

I had hoped to raise my son to be a good fishing buddy, but he had less staying power. His version is he was not as obsessed. My daughter also refuses to go fishing with me on a regular basis. This aversion may stem from an early childhood experience. Something to do with me changing her diapers on the frosty hood of our 67' Saab while waiting for the fog to burn off the Crooked River so the mayfly hatch would come out?

My mother has turned out to be a good partner on the stream. Note I didn't say fishing buddy because she doesn't fish. Mom is more than happy to wander around looking for tiny birds in the brush while I fish. When we meet on the trail, she admires my catch and I listen to her bird stories. She's also good about meeting at a pre-arranged location and is always on time. She knows I would leave her behind otherwise. It was a tough lesson for her to learn the first few times out, but she's a better person for it now.

Henry David Thoreau had it right when he wrote, "I have never found a companion that was so companionable as solitude." I couldn't agree more having yet to feel lonely on the water. That said, I don't mind sharing the water after I get my limit. I'll even net a fish for you on occasion. It's just that sometimes I like to fish when I want, where I want and how I want. Two is a crowd. I don't mind seeing you, but not in my fishing hole. Please go away.

Made in the USA
Monee, IL
01 October 2020